WIN THE WAR FOR MONEY & SUCCESS

BY

NEIL JESANI

Cataloging in Publication (Library of Congress)

Jesani, Neil, author

Win the War for Money & Success

Issued in print and electronic formats.

ISBN 978-1-7339303-9-0 (Paperback) ISBN 978-1-7339303-2-1 (eBook)

ISBN 978-1-7339303-5-2 (Audio Book)

Limit of Liability & Disclaimer: While the publisher and author have used their best efforts in preparing this book, they make no representation or warranties with respect to the accuracy or completeness of the contents of this book and specifically disclaim any express or implied warranties or fitness for a particular purpose, situation or individual. No warranty may be created by the sales and promotion efforts either online, offline or in-person.

Nothing in this publication constitutes investment or legal advice. It is in your best interest and is your responsibility to evaluate the accuracy and completeness of any opinions, advice, services or other information provided in this presentation. All information contained on any page is distributed with the understanding that the author, publisher and distributors are not rendering legal, accounting or other professional advice or opinions on specific facts or matters, and accordingly assume no liability whatsoever in connection with its use.

Please visit www.neiljesani.com for any questions, concerns, feedback, support, media or speaking engagement requests.

Special discounts on bulk quantities of this book are available for corporations, professional associations, trade unions or friends and family at www.neiljesani.com.

Neil Jesani, CFP
BeamaLife Corporation
100 Commons Way, Suite 250
Holmdel, NJ 07733
Phone: (732) 508-7415
www.BeamaLife.com

To the love of my life, my wife and super-woman Shalima, and two stars of my eyes – my daughter, Raniya, and son, Xavier. Thank you for putting up with me so far.

Contents

Preface

I grew up in a small town in India, in a lower-middle class family. It was a happy-go-lucky family with only one bill to pay every month and that was the electricity bill – that was it. No other bills or taxes to pay every month. There was not much in savings. I had never heard of insurance and the only investments we ever made were in the goods for our small business. I learned some basics of business and finance from the small family business but it was my formal education, as well as meeting the right people along the way and the habit of reading, that changed my life and helped me to become a successful financial planner. Certainly, God has been very kind throughout!

Over my last twenty years in the world of finance, I've realized that most people can't comprehend the complicated nature of investments, insurance, banking and other financial concepts. It's not their fault, of course. There are so many things to understand, process, and finally to make sense of. In fact, most financial professionals I've met don't understand them either.

Ironically, the financial services industry has contributed lots of information (and misinformation) in order to advance its own agenda. Also, the current model of distributing financial products and services is paradoxical. The most powerful financial people in the world design the most complicated financial concepts and products. These are ultimately delivered by mostly commission-based, generally less clever individuals. The folks at the top convince these financial sales people (you can call them brokers, agents, financial advisors, financial planners, financial consultants, personal bankers or any other name you like) to sell or distribute whatever the folks at the top are designing or producing.

Historically, the media has played and continues to play a vital role in any society. Various business or industry lobbyists have used the media to their own strategic advantage – some by being in the news all the time and others by staying under the radar. Today, it is very easy to find lots of information about any financial topic you can think of. But the hardest part is knowing what is the right choice for one's particular situation, what is the wrong choice, and what is the best information available that can help you.

Economically, I divide our society into four segments: 1) Lower-income people who live near the poverty line, 2) Middle-income earners, 3) Higher-income earners and 4) the Ultra-wealthy who deal in billions of dollars. Unfortunately, the lower-income segment does not have any means to implement financial strategies and they tend to pay lower or no taxes. They also tend to be the primary recipients of government entitlement programs, as they have the most need. The ultra-wealthy on the other hand will never run out of money, and they can very well influence the system in their favor to lower their tax burden, and create additional wealth building opportunities.

It's the folks in-between, the middle- and higher-income earners, who are in the greatest danger of paying more than their fair share of taxes, running out of money, or leaving their family in despair because of bad financial decisions and general misinformation. They are at war against higher taxes and unfair financial disadvantages, at war against a system that is designed to take their money, penalizing them for the results of their success. They studied well and worked hard to become as successfu as they can be. Taxes, inflation, market fluctuations, rising expenses, lawsuits and mediocre financial products, and advice are eroding their wealth and eating away at anything they might pass down as an inheritance to their family. If you are in the middle – paying more than your fair share of taxes and expenses, and having less and less to show for it – this book is for you.

I've always been shy and rather intimidated about sharing publicly the financial strategies I've learned over the last twenty years. During my career, I have helped more than 4,000 doctors, 3,000 successful small business owners, and many other senior professionals with the knowledge contained in this book. My clients and I typically talked in private settings, and they were receptive to my guidance and advice, and I'm pleased to say they were more successful reaching their goals as a result. My faith teaches me that if I am fortunate enough to get a higher education or become the beneficiary of great wisdom, then I'm called to share that knowledge with others, serving the community at large and continuing to discover God's creation, rather than only accumulating wealth for personal gain. These teachings finally convinced me to share my strategies and learnings with a larger audience, even though this might not be the typical approach of financial strategists.

And so this book was born.

While it will certainly benefit higher-income earners and high-net-worth individuals, it will also provide a solid pathway for people who aren't there yet, and aspire to improve their financial situation.

I always believe in discussions based on empirical evidence rather than someone's opinion. That is why I have tried to limit my opinions in this book. Instead, I provide as many facts and sources as possible. I hope this book is a good starting point in your financial strategies research and journey to lowering your taxes, enhancing your investment return, doubling your retirement income and potentially creating a legacy for generations to come. Ultimately, I hope it helps you win the war for money and success.

Introduction

Welcome to *Win the War For Money and Success.* This self-help financial book will help you understand some of the most important financial concepts and strategies to reduce taxes, create a better investment portfolio, potentially double your retirement income and, finally, to create a substantial inheritance for your loved ones or favorite charity.

The first three chapters of this book talk about taxes in general and some tax reduction strategies. The second and third chapters are primarily designed for the self-employed or aspiring self-employed, professionals, and small business owners. I am assuming most of you will have an accountant to help you with your taxes, so we'll look at the tax strategies generally beyond an accountant's scope.

Chapter 4 to Chapter 10 focus on understanding the real world of investments and money principles. It will be a good read for anyone, and I believe it will surprise you with some little-known facts and insights. It will provide you the basic framework for any investment decision going forward in your life. Investment decisions might seem small today, but they can have a far-reaching impact later on in your life. I want to help you be on the right path from the beginning.

The final four chapters provide you with practical strategies to implement some of the most common financial planning concepts. Chapter 11 covers estate planning, and even though the financial threshold for estate tax is fairly high, we'll cover some basic estate planning documents required in most situations.

Chapter 12 talks about individual private pension plans, which should be of great interest to both the self-employed and W2 employees alike. The information will help you implement a solid tax-reduction strategy and create guaranteed retirement income. Ultimately, the purpose of any long-term savings and investment is to create retirement income, liquidity and an inheritance for the family.

Chapter 13 will be primarily useful to parents and grandparents interested in saving for future college costs. Finally, Chapter 14 is geared towards people who are near or at retirement. However, it will include useful information for everyone who wants to be able to enjoy the golden years, have a higher retirement income and leave an inheritance.

Even though the book is arranged in chapters, it's designed for the reader to be able to skip around to any chapter, depending on the information they need most right now. I hope you'll keep coming back to this book again and again as your life needs change.

CHAPTER 1

Taxes, Taxes & Taxes

"The hardest thing to understand in the world is the income tax."

Albert Einstein

Before 1862, a worker in the United States could keep every dime they earned without worrying about paying a certain amount of those earnings to the government in taxes. Sounds wonderful, doesn't it? It didn't matter if you cleaned the stables or owned a large company. Your income was yours.

The Civil War changed this worker's paradise. Congress enacted the country's first income tax to pay for the war effort. Even back then, the government established it along the same lines as we know today. Two of its central principles were that the government based the first income tax on progressive or graduated taxation, and that the money would be withheld at the source of the income. Progressive means that the more you make, the greater the percentage of your income you have to give to the government.

As much as this was a shocking blow to the average citizen in 1862, we would take those tax rates today. The initial tax table had people who earned $600 to $10,000 a year contributing at a tax rate of 3%. People who made over $10,000 (in today's dollars, that's about $237,000) paid at a higher rate. This particular act that initiated the federal income tax also brought everyone's favorite agency into existence, the Commissioner of Internal Revenue. The early mandate of that government department was pretty much the same as it is now: to assess, levy, and collect all federal taxes. Even back then, they could enforce the tax laws by prosecuting somebody who owed the government, and seizing property and income.

This incarnation of the federal income tax ended in 1872 as Congress sought different income streams to fund the government. It had a brief reincarnation in 1894 and 1895 until the United States Supreme Court declared it unconstitutional. In order to get around this technicality, the 16th Amendment to the Constitution made the income tax a permanent component of the U.S. tax system. The amendment passed in 1913 and it gave Congress the legal authority to tax the income of both individuals and corporations.

Another war brought the last pieces of the puzzle together. Employment increased tremendously during World War II, as did the need for more tax dollars to pay for that mammoth endeavor. Congress introduced a withholding tax on wages in 1943. It exponentially increased the number of taxpayers and the amount of revenue generated. Not one to put a halt to a good thing, the United States has basically kept this system in place ever since.

While no individual is exempt from the federal income tax, the highest tax rate has been all over the charts. After World War II, the top marginal rate for people with high incomes was 90%! It stayed that way for years and dropped down to 70% in the 1960's. It was then lowered to 50% in the 1980's and came down to a low of 28% in 1988. Today, in 2019, it is 37%.

Top Federal Tax Rates

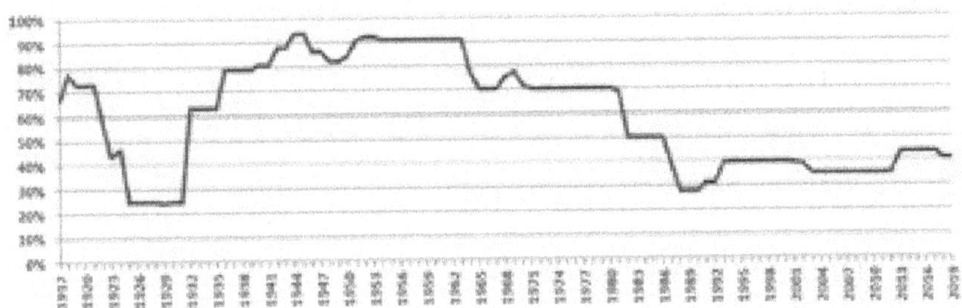

The bottom line is that if you have a significant income resulting from your profession or business, you are likely being taxed at the higher end of this scale. You are paying the United States government a fair amount of the money you earn. While You may not be learning anything new here, it is good to have a basic understanding of how the income tax came about, how it works, and why it is not ever going to go away.

But wait…there's more!

Not only do all workers pay taxes to the federal government based on their income, most also pay another income tax to the state they live in. Unless you are one of the lucky individuals who lives in Alaska, Florida, Nevada, South Dakota, Texas, New Hampshire, Washington, or Wyoming, you are paying a state income tax. Rates and filing complexity vary among the other 42 states where you pay more of your income to state taxes. You add this to what you send to the federal government, and the resulting figure goes even higher. The 10 highest income tax states for 2019 are:

1. California 13.3%

2. Hawaii 11%

3. Oregon 9.9%

4. Minnesota 9.85%

5. Iowa 8.98%

6. New Jersey 8.97%

7. Vermont 8.95%

8. District of Columbia 8.95%

9. New York 8.82%

10. Wisconsin 7.65%

But wait...there's still more!

Many cities and towns also modified their tax laws so that residents and/or people who work within their borders have to fork over some of their income. Using the 2019 New York City tax schedule as an example, the tax rates in the five boroughs of the city range from 3.078% to 3.876% of a person's income. It isn't just major cities that do this either. As tax dollars get harder and harder to come by, this method is a great way for local municipalities to supplement their income through local property and business taxes. For many Americans, it is quite possible to have three different government entities with their hands out, taking a piece of your hard-earned earnings.

And we're not done yet!

Another tax that we pay to the federal government is also based on our income. This one started with the Social Security Act of 1935. The stock market crash of 1929, and the resulting depression showed how people could be completely wiped out of any savings they might have built up over a lifetime. President Franklin D. Roosevelt championed the cause of a government-sponsored plan that would guarantee older Americans some sort of income if they became disabled or their working days were behind them.

Social Security was born. The funding the plan came from a percentage of workers' wages and salaries.

The original 14-page document that launched the Social Security Administration has greatly evolved since 1935. For one thing, it now includes paying for Medicare, which is hospital and medical care for the elderly and disabled. Paying for Social Security and Medicare comes under the banner of FICA. This stands for the Federal Insurance Contributions Act. Unlike the graduated method of the federal income tax, the FICA tax is a regressive tax on income. This means that everybody pays the same rate no matter your income. There is no standard deduction or personal exemption deduction.

The other major difference with FICA is that two entities pay into the tax. The employee and the employer pay an equal amount of money into FICA. If you are self-employed, that means that you are responsible for each half of the tax. If you are a salaried or hourly employee, part of your business expense is paying the employer version of the FICA tax.

The majority of FICA goes to Social Security. The only good news is that the Social Security portion of the tax is capped to a certain income level. Once you reach that level of income for the year, you no longer have to pay the Social Security piece of FICA, though the Medicare part continues.

To illustrate how this works, let's look at the numbers for 2019. The FICA tax breaks down so that the employer and employee each pay 6.2% of a person's wages or salary into Social Security. Once a person hits $132,900 in earnings, he or she stops paying for the Social Security piece until January 1, when the new year begins. For Medicare, the rate is 1.45% for both employee and employer, and that continues no matter what a person makes. That means up to the time someone makes $132,900, that person is paying 7.65% of their income into FICA. This money comes right off the top and you have no deductions or recourse to get any of it back. If the government runs it correctly, you will see some of it when you retire! Now if you are self-employed, you pay the combined employee and employer amount, which is a

12.4% Social Security tax on up to $132,900 of your net earnings and a 2.9% Medicare tax on your entire net earnings. If your earned income is more than $200,000 ($250,000 for married couples filing jointly), you must pay 0.9% more in Medicare taxes.

Now the purpose of this book is not to overwhelm you with the fact that we all pay a great deal of what we make into taxes. Truthfully, if you dwell on that fact every morning, the tendency is to cover up under the blankets and not get out of bed. This does not even touch on the other taxes you have in life such as property taxes, sales and excise taxes, estate and gift taxes

What we are going to look at in-depth for the rest of this book is how to save money on one of your biggest payments – the income tax that you send to the various governments. The tax laws are full of loopholes and nuances that are almost impossible to keep track of. For one thing, they are constantly changing, as we have seen in the Tax Cuts and Jobs Act of 2017. The other factor is that many aspects of the tax code only affect certain individuals or income levels. So it is important to know how you fit into the maze of codes, regulations and statutes.

There is a variety of ways to take large deductions when you own your own business and make a substantial income. These greatly reduce your annual tax burden. Besides making an immediate impact on what you pay the federal government each year, you will be hanging onto more of your money so that it will be there when you are ready to retire or move on from what you do now. Like so many strategies in our personal finances, one size doesn't fit all. We will look at a variety of programs that you can weigh against your own personal situation. Here is one last word on financial professionals. Not everyone knows everything. This is true in all walks of life and you have to take the time to know the background of the person you're working with. For example, Certified Public Accountants are fantastic at making sure your books are correct, and that all the proper filing is done for taxes and other financial matters. While their knowledge is broad, please do not assume that they are familiar with everything that can benefit you in terms of saving on your taxes. They certainly know how to keep an accurate accounting of your income, savings, and deductions, but they do not have the time or training to know the intricacies of all the programs available to you.

The same is true of tax attorneys. They certainly should know the pertinent laws, but they are not experts on investment-based tax strategies unless they have taken the necessary training. One area that many people err in is taking advice from the wrong — or less than competent — professional. Your finances are going to be complex, and many times you are asking questions as different as apples and oranges. Make sure the professional you talk to is well versed in apples if you are asking an apple question and the same for the oranges!

Ideally, you want to put a good team together to navigate the cross currents of your personal finances. When running your own business, or when reaching a certain income threshold, you are going to need a CPA to make sure your accounts and paperwork are correct. Depending on the complexity of your business and/or estate, you might want a tax or estate attorney for the necessary help. For figuring out how to invest and receive the most potential tax savings right now and for the future, talk to a certified financial planner with the specialized training, experience, and a track record of successfully helping others in a similar situation.

As we have seen from this introductory chapter, people pay a great deal of money to the government. It is bad enough when you work for a company and your employer has the responsibility of taking the necessary deductions out of your paycheck. However, if you own your own business, the responsibility to make sure your taxes are up to snuff falls squarely on your shoulders. As you read the rest of this book, we are going to look at the options you have to make this process as simple as possible. More importantly, we are going to see how you can keep significantly more of what you own, rather than handing it over to the United States government.

CHAPTER 2

Taxation of Various Business Structures

"For a nation to try to tax itself into prosperity is like a man standing in a bucket and trying to lift himself up by the handle."

Winston Churchill

When you are establishing your own business, there are many things to consider. It is important to put together as thorough a business plan as possible. Ideally, you should do this even before you sell your first item, see your first client, or treat your first patient. The reality is that this isn't always the case and many business owners practically have to reboot their business to align it in a manner that allows them to operate at an optimal level. It is okay to do this if you are already up and running. Sometimes a new business owner needs to get some experience under his or her belt to realize the areas they need to improve in order to strengthen their operations, cash flow, and income.

While a great business plan consists of many components, we're going to focus our attention on the ones affecting how your income is taxed. Often when somebody starts out in business, they do not anticipate the issues they will face as the company becomes bigger and more money pours into the business coffers. If you are just starting out establishing your own company, think about how you want to set your business up. However, if you have been operating already, it is perfectly fine to make changes if you believe that it is going to be advantageous for you.

One of the biggest questions facing most business owners is deciding what form of corporation will fit their needs best. This is an important consideration because how you establish your business determines how the Internal Revenue Service taxes your income. In fact, the IRS is one of the government entities you have to file with when you are starting out.

Many first-time business owners start out their companies as a sole proprietorship. Sometimes people do this because they really aren't sure where their business is headed. It might be something a person only wants to do part-time, or it is a start-up with no clear vision of success. It is also the easiest one to establish in terms of paperwork. All you have to do is send a form into the IRS requesting an Employer Identification Number (EIN) and you've created your own company. Depending where you live, there may be other things you need to do, such as registering the name of your company or filing local paperwork. For the most part, once you have that EIN, you are good to go.

Taxation as a sole proprietor is very straightforward. All of your net proceeds are taxed as individual income. The negative aspect of sole proprietorship is that you are exposing your personal assets to business liabilities. Nowadays, it is very easy to create and maintain a corporation, and often it is a mistake not to incorporate.

Let's look at several options you have when deciding what type of business structure you want to adopt. Generally speaking, there are three main choices when deciding on the ideal structure for your company. As we will see, they all have their pros and cons. Here is a broad picture of each of them, including the tax considerations.

S Corporation

First, we will look at an "S corporation." This is a typical corporation with a special tax designation by the IRS. As with any corporation, an owner files the necessary paperwork with the state along with all the appropriate fees. All states have websites to get the particular documentation for corporations established within their borders. Most states have departments to help guide businesses through the maze of paperwork and fees to become established.

Let's look at the tax considerations of an S corporation first. It is a standard corporation that has elected a special tax status with the IRS. Unlike a C corporation, which we will talk about next, an S corporation (S corp) does not pay any tax at the corporate level. What happens is that the profits of the company (or losses) are passed through to the shareholders. They in turn report this income or loss on their individual tax returns. For any tax that needs to be paid, it is done according to the individual's rates.

An S corporation is something to consider if you want the advantages of a corporation, but do not want to worry about dealing with a corporate tax and the income tax. One of the biggest reasons for incorporating your business is the limiting of your liability. By having your company under the auspices of a corporation, if a patient, client or customer sues you, then your personal property and savings are protected.

It is important to keep in mind that forming a corporation for your business will not protect you from professional errors. For example, if you are a doctor and a patient comes in to your office, slips on the floor, and injures his or herself in the fall, you have liability protection. However, if you do not treat a patient properly and he or she has future complications, your corporation will not protect you. This is no small consideration in our lawsuit happy world. This is a component of incorporating no matter which form you choose.

There are also other benefits with forming an S corporation. It provides alternatives to set salaries for the owners and employees, which helps you minimize the FICA tax. There also are accounting considerations. Most corporations must use the accrual accounting method unless they are considered a small corporation, which means the company has less than $5 million in annual gross receipts. Most S corporations fall into this area and do not use the accrual method unless they are a business that carries inventory. The reason this can be important is that accrual accounting can be a bit complex and can cost more to maintain.

Statistically, an S corporation has a lower chance of an IRS audit. S corporations file something called the informational tax return (Form 1120 S U.S. Income Tax Return for an S Corporation). Apparently, the IRS audits more companies when business income is only reported on Schedule C of Form 1040 on an individual's tax return.

In terms of the structure of an S corporation, it can have no more than 100 shareholders. Those shareholders have to be United States citizens and residents. Furthermore, a corporation, partnership, or trust cannot own an S corporation. There is only one class of stock and all shareholders must agree in writing to accepting the S corporation designation.

To summarize the S corporation, it avoids the double taxation of the corporate tax and allows the pass-through of profits and losses. Because the initial years of establishing a business have many start-up expenses that become tax losses, many businesses start out as an S corp, and may decide to change to a C corporation down the road. We'll talk more about C corporations in a moment.

One of the downsides to an S corporation is if the owners (stockholders) are in a high-income bracket, then their share of profits will be taxed at that high rate. While we will be looking at how to reduce that tax burden throughout this book, it is a consideration to keep in mind.

One other negative to an S corporation occurs when you are a high net-worth individual and doing your estate planning. If, later in life, you create a trust during the estate planning process to hold your company, S corporations are ineligible to be owned by a trust.

In summary, if you think your business should incorporate as an S corporation the main components you need to consider include:

1. It has to be a domestic corporation (headquartered in the United States).

2. Have no more than one hundred shareholders (none can be nonresident aliens, corporations, or trusts).

3. All shareholders consent to becoming an S corp.

4. Have one class of stock.

5. File the necessary paperwork with the IRS (Form 2553) and be approved by the IRS.

C Corporation

Now, a C corporation is more like what most of us think of as the standard corporation. Like the S corp, you file the necessary documents and pay the filing fee with a state to form a C corporation. The framework of a C corporation dictates that the personal liability for the corporation's business debts is limited to how much money each shareholder puts into the company.

One of the biggest differences between an S and C corporation is in the area of taxation. The C corporation or C corp is considered its own entity and thus has to file a corporate tax return to report its losses or profits. If there are profits, they are then taxed at the current corporate level (approximately 21% in 2019). Losses do not pass through to the shareholders to use as a deduction against other income. In fact, the profits of the C corporation can be "double taxed." Besides the corporate tax on profits, any dividends passed onto shareholders are reportable income and the individuals have to pay taxes on them at whatever their current rate is. In other words, the profits are taxed at the corporate level and again on the individual's tax return.

Besides the double taxation by the federal government, many states also have an income tax that only applies to C corporations and applies to all income over a certain amount. In many cases, that means profits from a C corp are taxed three times – twice by the feds and once by the state. Throw in states with their own personal income tax, and those dividends received by a stockholder, may be skimmed for the fourth time.

All that said, there are many reasons a C corporation might be the right way for a company to go. The C corporation has fewer restrictions in terms of its establishment than an S corp. For one thing, it can have an unlimited number of shareholders. Those shareholders can be from outside the United States as well as being other corporations, partnerships, or trusts. Because of this, it puts the company in a better position to raise venture capital for funding or to take the company public. You can have several classes of stock in a C corporation as opposed to only one with an S corp, and the C corporation gives different profit-sharing options to its stockholders. This enables more profits to stay within the company to foster growth.

In terms of tax planning, you can see how a C corporation can spread the earnings between the company and shareholders. Like the S corporation, a C corp gives greater flexibility over structuring salaries and benefits for the owners and the employees. It is also simpler to set up expense accounts for travel and entertainment as well as offering stock options to employees.

Some of the downsides with a C corporation are that it must file a tax return every year with the IRS. This has to be done even if the company had no income. The additional tax filings and complex bookkeeping means more accounting work in a C corp. As mentioned earlier, some states have a state corporate income tax. Corporations with employees are required to pay federal (and sometimes state) payroll and unemployment taxes.

Here is one last note on the C and S corporations. All corporations are C corporations unless they specifically elect to become S corporations.

Limited Liability Company (LLC)

An LLC is a type of a business structure that combines the best of the S and C corporation. It is a way of organizing your company so that a business owner (or owners) can limit their liability while maintaining pass-through. An LLC is not subject to a corporate tax, and an owner's personal savings and property are protected. In terms of income tax, the profits and losses of an LLC pass through to the owners and are then paid on their individual income taxes.

An LLC is formed by the proper filing of documents and paying the state fees. The paperwork and obligations required to form an LLC are considerably less than an S or C corporation. It eliminates the drawbacks of an S corporation while maintaining the benefits of an S corporation. There are different reasons that a business owner may want to take this approach with his or her company.

One consideration is that if you anticipate losses for at least two years, you can pass this loss to yourself and any other owners. This will have a significant beneficial impact on your personal income tax. Also, an LLC can own real estate and can give you a great deal of flexibility in determining your management structure, accounting process, and reducing your organizational formalities. An LLC is not subject to holding to a set schedule of meetings for directors or keeping detailed records for all major business decisions. Corporations need to hold annual meetings, keep minutes, and carefully document pretty much everything. An LLC is a much looser structure to administer.

Professional Corporations (PC) & Professional Limited Liability Corporations (PLLC)

Licensed professionals have two other options for the structure of their business, called Professional Corporations (PC) or Professional Limited Liability Corporations (PLLC), and these have some specific advantages. In a Professional Corporation, only professionals licensed in whatever their specialty is can be the shareholders. For instance, you can have a group of doctors, a group of lawyers, etc. as shareholders. But remember — only members of the profession are the shareholders; there are no exceptions. For example: A doctor's brother who is not a licensed physician cannot be a shareholder. The corporate organization of a PC allows its shareholders to have more direct control over managing its operations.

Professional Limited Liability Corporations are only allowed in certain states that established laws to form them. These are easier to set up than a regular corporation and have easier operational guidelines. However, not all states have these and if you are looking to operate in multiple states, you need to check if the PLLC is allowed where you want to establish offices or subsidies.

Both a PC and a PLLC have such similar features that it is difficult to tell them apart. Taxation is one area where they differ. The PLLC has pass-through taxation. A PC also allows pass-through taxation if it files as an S corp; otherwise, it will be taxed as a C corp at the maximum corporate rate of 21 percent. When deciding to go with a PC or PLLC, it is important to weigh all of the pros and cons, including the state of residence and taxation options.

Selection of State to Incorporate

When setting up a corporation, the topic of what state to establish in usually comes up. This is definitely something that you need to research, especially if you are planning to grow faster and bring in outside investments. For the most part, it comes down to the ease of filing the documents and the fees involved. States like Delaware and Nevada are popular for filing because it is a fairly simple task compared to other states. Often, that is the only advantage. If you form your corporation in one state but operate in another, you are still subject to the taxes and regulations of the state you are physically located in.

Summary

This brings us back to one of the main points from the beginning of the chapter. This is a very general outline of the various advantages and disadvantages of forming a corporation or LLC for your business. Terms like LLC, C corp, PLLC, etc. are thrown around a great deal, but a business owner often doesn't think about or have time to look into the options for how to establish a company. Hopefully, this chapter gave you some food for thought and helpful guidance as you establish or expand your business.

In very broad general terms, for a typical professional company, an LLC incorporated as an S corporation offers the flexibility and tax savings that many desire. It will be a perfect option for estate planning purposes later on. You need to do the necessary research on your own or discuss the option that is best for you with a qualified professional.

Now that we have looked at ways to organize your business, we are going to move into more detail on how to reduce the amount of money you pay to the government in taxes every year. The great thing is that you can position yourself for both short-term and long-term gain. That is not usually an option we have for many things in life.

CHAPTER 3

Retirement Plans – A Big Tax Reduction Vehicle

"There may be liberty and justice for all, but there are tax breaks only for some."

Martin A. Sullivan

Most of us do not want to work all of our lives. At the same time, not too many people look forward to retirement as just sitting on the front porch watching life go by. With people staying healthy longer and a zest for life increasing with age, many look at retirement as a way to do even more. This might mean travel, starting or working for a charity you believe in, hitting a golf course in every state, or even starting a completely different business than the one you worked in for the last 30 years. Whatever a person's desires, having a decent amount of money saved up to finance those dreams is imperative.

We spent the last chapter looking at how to establish a company in a manner that will work best for you in terms of structure and tax considerations. Next, we want to look at how to reduce those income tax obligations. What fits very nicely is that here is a case in your personal business where you can truly kill two birds with one stone. That is because one of the best ways to maximize your income tax deductions will also secure a very successful retirement!

A skilled CPA will help you determine business deductions. If you own your own business, you will have many. A problem occurs when you reach that threshold of "success." When your business thrives and your gross revenues are growing, your business deductions are only going to do so much for you. This is the opportune time in your career to start planning for what happens when your working days are done. While that may seem far away, the brilliant component of starting your retirement fund now is that you will begin to realize sizable tax deductions that will keep more money in your pocket now and in the future.

The history of setting up retirement plans in the United States started in 1875 when the American Express Company established the first private pension plan in an effort to create a stable, loyal workforce. Since that time, retirement plans have gone through a long evolution in both the government sector in terms of regulations, and with finance companies in how they construct plans. Both sides of the aisle are always tweaking laws and programs to serve the workforce. In the case of a small business, the owner and owner's family are the primary workforce.

To summarize before we go into detail, there are several ways to invest your money in retirement plans. While there are limits to the amount you can put into a plan each year, the money you place into a qualified account is totally tax deductible.

All retirement plans have their own particular structure and regulations. In general, the money you put away for retirement is not available until you reach a certain age, usually 59.5. Many do have provisions for early withdrawal criteria, but there is usually a penalty. When withdrawing from a retirement plan after retirement age, you will pay taxes on that money and whatever it earned when you take it out. Typically, you will be in a lower tax bracket after retiring, so that money will be taxed at a lower rate than it would be now.

Types of Retirement Plans

The retirement plans we are examining here are the "qualified" plans. That means they are IRS approved and your contributions are tax deductible. We will discuss different ones, as there are choices that you can make that will best fit your situation. Non-qualified retirement plans would include a deferred compensation plan, Section 162 executive bonus plan, or Section 7702 private pension using cash value life insurance. While some of these vehicles have earnings that may be tax deferred, you cannot take any tax deductions for the contributions you make to them unless the cash value life insurance purchased was in a qualified plan.

There are two broad categories of qualified retirement plans that a business owner can utilize. One is the defined contribution plan and the other is the defined benefit plan. As their names imply, they both work within IRS limits to determine how much can go into the plan each year. These plans have different components that a business owner has to weigh to determine what fits their situation best. Examples of qualified plans are profit sharing plans, a SEP plan, defined benefit plan, solo-defined benefit plan, 412i defined benefit plan, and the cash balance plan. If that seems confusing, don't worry. In the next chapters, we will look at specific ways these plans can be set up in terms of the investment aspect for the money, but we will now look at the two categories of qualified plans.

Defined Contribution Plans

As the name suggests, in this plan, IRS has defined the contribution you make. For example, you would contribute the lesser of $56,000 or 25% of your FICA eligible compensation into your defined contribution plan for the year 2019. To illustrate, a business owner makes $200,000 in W2 income from his or her business. That business owner could contribute the lower of $56,000 or 25% of his or her total compensation, which was $200,000 for the year. Since that amount would total $50,000, the lower amount of $50,000 is all they could place in their defined contribution plan. These defined contribution plans include profit sharing and IRA-based SEP plans.

SEP is an acronym for Simplified Employee Pension. This retirement plan is especially ideal for a self-employed business owner. The costs are low, the administration is easy, and, as mentioned, you can contribute that 25% of your compensation or $56,000, whichever is lower. The implementation costs and paperwork for starting a SEP are minimal. In fact, the annual operating costs for a SEP are low as compared to other types of plans. Any size business can establish a SEP, and there is no filing requirement for the employer.

If you have employees, the downside with a SEP is you also have to make the same contribution to their accounts as you do for yours: the lower amount of 25% of their salary, or $56,000. If you have an employee that is 21 year old, worked for your business in at least 3 of the last 5 years and received at least $600 in compensation, you are required to pay into a SEP plan for them.

Let's say Lori is your office manager, and you pay her $40,000/year. At the three-year mark, she needs to go onto your SEP plan, and you will have to pay an additional $10,000 into the plan on her behalf in addition to her salary. Furthermore, there is no vesting schedule requirement on a SEP plan. If Lori takes another position after you pay into her plan during the first year of her eligibility, she can take all that money with her.

A word on vesting here, because it leads into the next topic, the Profit Sharing plan. Vesting is the amount of time an employee needs to wait before they can access a partial or total amount of their pension plan. An employer can establish two vesting options with a pension plan. One is "cliff vesting" where the employee is not eligible to withdraw any of their pension money for at least three years of being employed by that company; then they have 100% access. "Graded vesting" is when they are eligible for a certain percentage over their first five years. They are entitled to 20% after one year, 40% after two, and so on until they are 100% vested after five years.

As you saw, the SEP plan is fine if you are the only employee of your company, but definitely has other considerations if you employ others. With Profit Sharing, you have greater flexibility. It has the 25% of salary or the $56,000 limit (whichever is lower) that is a component of all defined contribution plans for the year 2019. While you still have to pay into the plan for other employees, the requirements are different from the SEP plan. Two years of working before they have to put into the plan still holds, but they also have to work at least 1,000 hours a year for you. Furthermore, the amount you need to put into the plan for them is subject to a different schedule so it will be lower. Finally, you can set a vesting schedule for the plan for all employees.

Correctly setting up and administering a Profit Sharing Plan is the key to its success, as well as meeting the regulations of the IRS and the Labor Department. If you, as a self-employed or a company owner, consider this option as the way to go for a retirement plan for yourself and your business, work with an expert in this field with a reputation of success as they can bring the best design to help you maximize the power of your money. It is important to establish such a program that meets all requirements and will run smoothly for you and your workers.

Finally, both defined benefit plans have a limitation of maximum $56,000 maximum deduction. If you are looking to contribute higher amounts than the current IRS limit of $56,000, then you should consider a defined benefit plan where you would be able to take a much higher income deduction and would be able to contribute much more for yourself.

Defined Benefit Plans

Until 1970, most large corporations used the defined benefit plan to guarantee the retirement of their employees. Today they are very popular among high income earning self-employed professionals like physicians, lawyers and business owners due to the many favorable changes in the tax code. For these successful self-employed professionals and business owners, a defined benefit plan is a big income tax deduction tool.

In a defined benefit plan, the IRS does not define the contribution made to the plan, but rather, the amount of the retirement benefit at the retirement age. A qualified pension actuary or attorney will take your current age and income to calculate your allowable retirement benefit when you reach age 65. In 2019, this amount is $225,000. The next step is to calculate the contribution amount to ensure this benefit at retirement. Contributions to the plan are calculated based on your current age, your highest income in the last three years, and the years left until your retirement. The pension actuary calculates the annual contribution needed to reach the benefit number, and you receive an income tax deduction for your annual contribution into the plan.

Essentially the biggest bonus to a defined benefit plan is that it will give you a significantly larger deduction — up to $350,000 — as compared to the maximum of the $56,000 you can place into a defined contribution plan.

New IRS rules make defined benefit plans very attractive. The government repealed Section 415(e) of the Tax Code. Because of this change in law, a business owner can now use a defined benefit plan to build assets without taking into consideration money already accumulated in other retirement plans. Other changes the IRS made were to Section 415(b)(1)(A) to increase the maximum retirement benefit allowed. Section 415(b)(2)(C) was amended to lower the age at which the maximum retirement benefit could be received.

In addition, the 2006 Pension Protection Act provides additional flexibility by allowing contributions of no more than 6.0% to a defined contribution plan, in addition to salary deferrals, *without* impacting the contribution to a defined benefit plan. The Tax Cuts and Jobs Act of 2017 added 20 percent qualified business income (QBI) deduction. Together, all these changes allow small business owners to contribute more to a defined benefit plan than ever before.

To show the power of a defined benefit plan, let's look at a successful pharmacy owner who is 48 years old. He is looking to take the highest income deduction possible and still allow himself a high degree of flexibility.

1. W-2 earnings: $235,000
2. Corporation profit: $350,000
3. Maximum Defined Benefit & 401(k) contribution: $189,000
4. Annual tax savings: (at 40% combined tax rate) $75,600

There are different designs of defined benefit pension plans. A cash balance plan is a type of defined benefit plan that resembles a defined contribution plan. For this reason, these plans are referred to as hybrid plans. A traditional defined benefit plan promises a fixed monthly benefit at retirement that is usually based upon a formula that takes into account the employee's compensation and years of service. A cash balance plan looks like a defined contribution plan because the employee's benefit is expressed as a hypothetical account balance instead of a monthly benefit.

The defined benefit plan also offers employers great flexibility in the scheduled amount and vesting requirements when offered to employees. The impact on taxes, how much you can put away for retirement, and the options it gives you in regards to your staff makes this plan worth looking into for your business.

Other Aggressive Tax Deduction Plans

There are some other aggressive retirement and benefit plans that could provide much higher income tax deductions, but they come with their own perils. Following are some examples:

- Captive Insurance Company
- Restricted Property Trust
- Delaware Statutory Trust
- Section 79 plan
- 419 plan

Summary

Pension plans are a great income tax and retirement planning tool to start with, but they require special expertise to get the maximum benefits possible. There are many IRS rules to be followed in regards to setting up the proper plan documents (including and excluding the employees, contribution limits to the plan, validating a plan and filing the annual 5500 pension tax return to IRS.)

You can see the incredible tax deductions that both the defined benefit plan, and to a lesser extent, the defined contribution plan provides. When you own a profitable business, no single deduction is going to knock more off your personal taxes than this approach without unnecessarily raising any red flags to the IRS. You save a great deal of money now, and are putting a large sum away for the future. In addition, the money you are investing will grow even bigger.

This chapter is meant to give you a basic understanding of the different retirement plans, and their short-term and long-term impact to your finances. This plan might be using tax-deduction tools primarily for self-employed and business owners, but there are some strategies such as IRS Section 7702 individual private pension plan that will work equally for W-2 employees and the self-employed.

Please keep in mind that this book was written in 2019. The amounts stated are current for 2019, but remember that they do change. Many of the limits talked about are subject to annual cost of living adjustments. While the basic information about the plans will not change much over time, it is always important to see what the current limits are for funding and tax deductions in any given year.

If your business or medical practice is successful, you should run the numbers on how much you will save in taxes, and how much you will accumulate for retirement over a twenty-, or even ten-year period. The amount will stagger you. The recent changes in the defined benefit plan have made this plan even work with large number of employees, while in the past it was meant to work with high income earner/owners with only few younger, low-income employees.

CHAPTER 4

Understanding the Intricate Nature of Money

"Successful investing is anticipating the anticipation of others."
John Maynard Keynes

Money has been around for a long time. Before its invention, early civilization worked on something of a barter system. As cultures advanced, so did the way they conducted business. Perhaps the first money was the Mesopotamian shekel from around 3000 BC. The Lydians first started minting coins around 650–600 BC. For centuries, money was based on a certain commodity, like gold or silver, and governments made currency from those metals. Early paper money was more of a promissory note based on the gold they represented. These days, money is simply backed by good faith in the government's ability to convert the money into goods via payment.

It is important to understand certain properties of money when you are spending it, saving it, or investing it. Many times, we think of money as a bunch of bundled up bills that just sit there. We also know that the more bundles, the better! However, money is not a stagnant object. It is very liquid, and an understanding of how this works with investments and savings is enlightening.

Velocity of Money

You have heard the old axiom when investing of, "Not to put all your eggs in one basket." This usually pertains to the wisdom of diversifying your investments in different areas to decrease the chances of any one investment not doing well. This is certainly true and we will be looking more at that in the next chapter. However, it also has another meaning. When you have money in one place, accumulating in one financial product, it is more susceptible to being eaten away by financial eroding factors such as fees, taxes, inflation, market dynamics, interest rate changes, and the performance of other investments. Think of it as a sitting target.

On the other hand, money in motion creates more money. The velocity of money obtains a multiplier effect and moves faster than the eroding factors. Money should serve multiple purposes. Banks use the same money over and over again. This concept is the "velocity of money." Let's look at a simple example to illustrate both sides of the equation.

You have $100,000 you want to put away. You decide to go the very safe route and put all of the money into a CD with a bank. The interest may be at an annual rate of 2%. For the most part, you will be taxed on whatever interest you earn on the CD. When taking out a CD, you are locked into a certain amount of time like one, three, or five years. For whatever the time period of your CD, you cannot do anything else with that money.

Now see what the bank does with your $100,000. It could lend $25,000 out to a small business where they charge 8% interest to the borrower. As that person begins to pay back that loan, the bank starts using the money somewhere else. Now start to multiply that scenario and you see what happens. Out of your original $100,000, the bank uses another $50,000 to fund a second mortgage for someone. Maybe $15,000 goes for a student loan and the remaining $10,000 helps fund the bank's credit card program. They lend all of your money out for a greater rate of interest than they are paying on your CD. As the money comes back in from those other loans, the bank immediately puts it to use elsewhere.

Banks also have a unique advantage because they are only required to have 10% of the funds in the bank in order to lend out 100%. A bank isn't really a safe holding everyone's savings; it is more of a revolving door where money doesn't sit still for very long. When all is said and done, the velocity of money means the bank earned 15-25% interest on your original $100,000 while paying you 2%!* That spread between your 2% and what they earned is how the bank pays for its staff, buildings, general overhead, etc., as well as making exponential profits. Money in motion makes more money.

Now I know that large financial institutions have the resources to do a lot more than an individual. However, you can take a lesson from how a bank multiplies its assets and puts your money to work in a variety of ways. It is possible for you to derive a multiplier effect on your money in other secure ways that are safe and dependable. That is, there are many ways to put your money into motion. Here are couple of quick visual examples of putting money into motion using what's called the "self-leveraging technique." There are many things that go into this technique and one needs to consider many factors before putting a strategy like this into practice.

*Plus 15-25% on its ability to lend out an additional $900,000 based on a 10% fractional reserve set by the Federal Reserve. Banks are more like slot machines that win 10 fold every time a coin is dropped into the machine. For more information read: https://www.managementstudyguide.com/how-fractional-reserve-banking-creates-money.htm.

Year	Age	POLICY PREMIUM	TAX FREE INCOME	SURRENDER VALUE	DEATH BENEFIT
1	48	300,000	0	90,081	4,183,000
2	49	300,000	0	381,457	6,475,535
3	50	300,000	0	695,339	6,782,402
4	51	300,000	0	1,028,364	7,112,418
5	52	300,000	0	1,385,298	7,466,156
6	53	0	0	1,475,782	5,950,000
7	54	0	0	1,572,771	5,920,000
8	55	0	0	1,709,951	2,950,000
9	56	0	0	1,855,534	2,950,000
10	57	0	0	2,010,149	3,054,842
11	58	0	0	2,174,608	3,165,739
12	59	0	0	2,349,346	3,279,839
13	60	0	0	2,551,459	3,418,902
14	61	0	0	2,739,134	3,561,134
15	62	0	0	**2,941,289**	3,764,830
16	63	0	0	3,158,138	3,979,506
17	64	0	0	3,391,655	4,205,638
18	65	0	0	3,641,267	4,443,565
19	66	0	0	3,911,355	4,683,426
20	67	0	0	4,200,079	4,998,095
21	68	0	400,000	4,087,403	4,898,736
22	69	0	400,000	3,971,500	4,795,365
23	70	0	400,000	3,858,962	4,687,780
24	71	0	400,000	3,742,809	4,575,768
25	72	0	400,000	3,627,021	4,480,237
26	73	0	400,000	3,551,888	4,312,350
27	74	0	400,000	3,398,148	4,051,745
28	75	0	400,000	3,287,813	3,797,948
29	76	0	400,000	3,179,621	3,570,152
30	77	0	400,000	3,074,702	3,492,571
31	78	0	400,000	2,971,858	3,419,843
32	79	0	400,000	2,874,667	3,352,660
33	80	0	400,000	2,780,779	3,291,790
34	81	0	400,000	2,691,828	3,237,991
35	82	0	400,000	2,608,254	3,191,896
			6,000,000		

POLICY PREMIUM		SELF LOAN & INCOME	POLICY VALUE	SURRENDER VALUE	DEATH BENEFIT
300,000		0	259,260	0	9,659,260
300,000		0	591,151	348,151	9,891,351
300,000		0	823,170	542,144	10,182,170
300,000		0	1,190,128	854,676	10,490,128
300,000		0	1,456,609	1,189,011	10,819,609
600,000	⇐	600,000	2,305,310	1,209,767	10,835,310
600,000	⇐	600,000	2,794,845	1,242,949	10,863,345
600,000	⇐	600,000	3,531,265	1,328,126	10,905,190
600,000	⇐	600,000	4,317,429	1,428,556	10,962,050
600,000	⇐	600,000	5,182,641	1,571,335	11,061,319
600,000	⇐	600,000	6,304,735	1,784,762	11,181,510
600,000	⇐	600,000	7,094,238	1,921,436	11,324,712
600,000	⇐	600,000	8,175,805	2,150,866	11,519,844
600,000	⇐	600,000	9,182,790	2,366,061	11,746,065
600,000	⇐	600,000	**10,570,653**	2,648,581	12,006,365
0		0	11,805,103	2,982,637	5,921,634
0		0	12,088,038	3,351,748	6,252,877
0		0	12,938,802	3,755,657	6,080,004
0		0	13,828,820	4,237,070	6,962,836
0		0	14,791,724	4,678,170	7,488,757
0		660,000	15,817,738	4,509,724	7,352,924
0		660,000	16,920,940	4,340,325	7,215,184
0		660,000	18,079,431	4,181,465	7,075,568
0		660,000	19,334,520	4,056,566	6,934,014
0		660,000	20,639,787	3,901,056	6,586,235
0		660,000	22,052,302	3,781,728	6,211,437
0		660,000	23,561,705	3,688,796	5,809,349
0		660,000	25,175,964	3,616,441	5,378,761
0		660,000	26,904,183	3,571,658	4,918,862
0		660,000	28,747,137	3,557,066	4,994,427
0		660,000	30,712,193	3,569,451	5,105,261
0		660,000	32,807,162	3,614,474	5,254,832
0		660,000	35,040,190	3,694,868	5,446,877
0		660,000	37,428,778	3,814,190	5,685,179
0		660,000	39,954,060	3,971,192	5,972,895
		9,900,000			

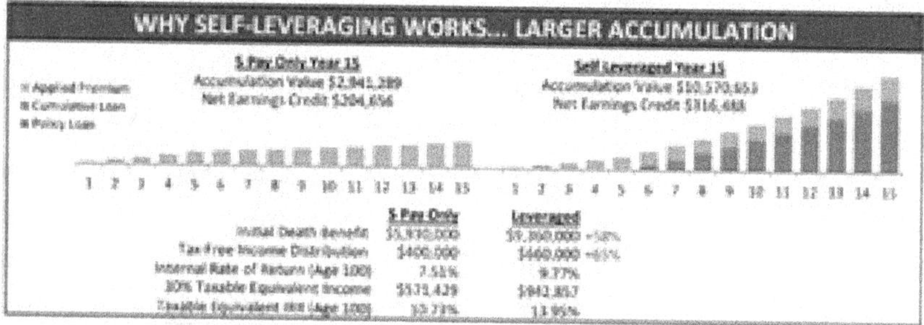

Here is another visual that shows the power of money in motion. You can put your existing savings and investments to second use by utilizing this strategy. Granted this illustration is meant for people with a certain income and net-worth but the concept works the same at any income level. It will be hard to understand without much context, and I do not want to take the entire chapter for this one topic, but it enhances your rate of return, creates tax-free income and minimizes the expenses of investments.

How You Use Money, Not Where You Put It

In the above example, I used only a few methods in which a bank takes your money and makes more money from it. In reality, there are many approaches to how a bank can lend out money in order to bring more into its coffers. The point is not so much what those methods are, but the fact that they utilize so many methods. If a bank used all of their money for home mortgages, their rate of return would not be much more than what they pay you for your CD. The bank may be able to operate this way, but if there is a downturn in the housing market, they might find themselves in trouble. That's why banks lend and invest in many different types of categories.

This is the approach you need to take with your money. It is there for you to use. The successful investor is more concerned with making the best use of his or her money rather than looking for that ideal investment to put it in.

What do I mean by this? Many people are always looking for that one hot stock or new company or great investment portfolio as a place to invest. That shiny object syndrome becomes their guiding principle in trying to increase their wealth. This philosophy means that the investor is looking to meet a certain need or goal based on what they learn about that particular product. Rather than focusing on that, it is more productive to concentrate on the method you use in investing.

Even if you are not a golfer, here is a simple analogy to illustrate this point. Some golfers are so sure that if they have the right clubs, or golf balls, or shoes that their game will improve dramatically. These players will think nothing of dropping $500 on the newest driver if they think it will let them hit the ball straighter and farther. Unfortunately, if he or she still hits the ball wrong with the new driver, they aren't going to do any better than they did with the old club. Rather than sinking money into equipment, the player would be better off working on his swing, or learning course management, or how to hit good shots after hitting a bad one.

Investing is the same. It is much more important to learn how to properly manage your money than it is learning where to put it. Don't get me wrong; it is important to know where you are putting your money. However, once you know how best to use your money, the easier it will be to evaluate where to invest it. Managing your finances does not occur in isolated segments, but organically, where all the factors you need to know work together.

Money Is Not Math, Money Is a Commodity

In general, a commodity is anything that can be bought and sold and has a value. Often the value fluctuates depending on supply and demand and an entire host of factors. The other fact about a commodity is that its value can erode over time.

Money is a commodity, just as much as wheat or iron is. When you use these commodities up, they are gone. If you are in a business that utilizes one of the two commodities I mentioned, you have to go out and look for more when what you have is gone. Without them, you can not bake bread or build automobiles. If you think of money in the same light, you will be ahead of most people on your way to securing financial success.

We know that money is a commodity. It changes in value and can erode over time. It is impossible in the end to keep constant the mathematical assumptions used in the calculations of money decisions today. The mathematical assumptions include interest rates, investment returns, tax rates, and inflation rates. These factors are certain to change and drastically affect our mathematical outcomes.

Let's bring this together in one more illustration. You have three peaches in a bowl in your kitchen. You go to the store, buy another half dozen, and add them to the bowl. How many do you have? The math is simple: 3 + 6 = 9. As a mathematical problem, it is simple to solve with arithmetic.

Now what if you left all those peaches there for ten years? How many would you have then? Mathematically you may still have nine, but in reality, odds are you would have none. A lot could happen to those peaches in that time. They might dry up and turn to dust. They could have been eaten before a week went by. The point is that they are a commodity that can deteriorate or erode over time. There are many different forces at work that could bring about a negative change to the peaches.

Your money is no different. Money is not stagnant. Its value can go up or down. Forces of economics, national money policies, and various other factors will affect your money over time. This concept is very important to understand as you read spreadsheets of how an investment performed, or you are looking at its future projections.

This is why we are spending a little time discussing the true value and nature of money. Too often, numbers are thrown around and it is easy to lose perspective of what they all mean. When you are dealing with your savings and investments, please keep in mind that those numbers represent a very real, significant amount of dollar bills. Never lose sight of that!

Average Return Is Not Actual Return

One of the sad truths in the financial world is that it is quite easy to manipulate numbers...and even math...to make something look better than it actually is. This is why you have to educate yourself on what you are reading or hearing about when evaluating an investment. While math is an absolute, it can be very easily used to give a false impression. Let's look at an example of figuring out the average rate of return on an investment.

For this example, you have $100,000 invested in a stock. In your first year, it does fantastic and you get 100% rate of return. You now have $200,000. Since it did so great, you let the money ride and the second year it loses 50%, and you are back to $100,000. You go one more year and it does another high earning of 100% rate of return. You are again at $200,000. Since you didn't learn your lesson from two years ago, you keep the money there, it suffers another minus 50% rate of return, and you are back to $100,000. In four years, you didn't make a dime.

However, let's look at the math. Over those four years, the *total* rate of return was 200%. You add together the two years of 50% losses and subtract the 100% from the 200%. Using that math, the money had a 100% rate of return over four years for an *average* rate of return over that period of 25% while the *actual* rate of return is 0%. Here is how it looks in the mathematical formula: 100% - 50% + 100% - 50% = 100%...100%/4 = 25%).

As you can see, while the math is correct, calculating investments take more than basic arithmetic. The investment industry uses a geometric means of calculating such things as average rate of return that utilizes other real -world factors so that the figures reflect close to reality.

Another concept an investor should know is the multiplier effect. Simply stated, if you sustain a 50% loss, you then need a 100% return just to make up that loss. This is illustrated in the example above. When the $200,000 got cut down to $100,000 in year 2 of the scenario, it took a 100% return the following year to get it back to the original $200,000.

One of the critical points of investing is how well you manage losses. They are going to happen. You need to have a strategy in place to limit potential losses and know how to react when it does happen.

As we continue discussing different investment strategies and products, look at numbers and statistics with a discerning eye. Quite often, numbers give you a snapshot of what is going on at one particular time. It doesn't necessarily mean it is true over an extended time frame.

Summary

As you can see, the concept of money is not as simple as you might have imagined. First of all, a dollar is a dollar. It has a very real value that you have to constantly be aware of. From there, money becomes very complex. It can do many different things, often at the same time. The crux of the problem is determining how to best use the money you have. While you are not a large financial institution, you have many different options on how to save and invest your money.

The concepts presented in this book are kept simple in order to present the complexities of saving and investing simply and understandably. As we are about to get into more specifics about investing and the various vehicles for doing so, you will see that each have their own particular traits. While it is important to understand them, they are impossible to master unless that is the business you are in.

CHAPTER 5

Factors Affecting Investment Return

"It is more difficult to win in a stock market than to compete in Olympics."

Ray Dalio

Now that you have a better understanding of the nature of money, you have to decide how to make it work best for you. There is no one answer to that question. As we saw in the last chapter, it isn't meant to be one answer, but many. There are so many factors involved including how much money you are working with, the time frame you are looking at, and your temperament when it comes to investing. A good rule of thumb is never do anything that prevents you from sleeping soundly.

With all of the ways to invest, you will discover different pros and cons for each type. As you get a handle on your strategy, you need to know the different types of investments, how each is taxed, and how much it costs you to invest in something. So there are three main factors that will affect your return on your investment:

- Asset Allocation
- Taxation
- Expenses

First Factor Affecting Return: Asset Allocation

This is where you do not put all of your eggs in one basket. You want to balance risk versus reward by having an investment portfolio with a certain percentage of your money going to each investment type that you decide on. This is where your risk tolerance, goals, and investment time frame come into play as you decide on your investments.

There are two kinds of investments we use for wealth building: 1) Short-term and 2) Long-term. The short-term wealth building investments are liquid assets, things like checking accounts, savings accounts, money markets and so forth for your emergencies, opportunities, security, and just overall peace of mind.

Before we look at the return of long-term investments, let's understand the underlying premise for all long-term investments. Why are we giving up current enjoyment of our income? The answer is to have a comfortable income stream in retirement and pass the left-over assets to family and charity in the most efficient way. It only makes sense then to understand how retirement income streams work so that we can direct today's savings in ways that potentially gives us the highest income when we retire.

In other words, how retirement income streams work defines how we should allocate our savings today. The sooner we get on an efficient path, the greater impact we will have on the results. There are two rates that make up everyone's retirement income stream later on, and both are equally important. One is the accumulation rate – getting up the mountain. The other is the distribution rate – getting back down safely. Knowing how retirement income streams work and then how distribution rates work, is the basis for understanding how to save money in pre-retirement.

While we will be looking at these in detail in subsequent chapters, here are some brief points about the various asset classes such as stocks, bonds, real estate, cash, commodities, and cash-value life insurance.

Stocks

In its simplest form, stock is ownership in a company. A business issues stocks to raise capital and you can own a certain amount of the company depending on how many shares you buy. You make money on the stock if the value goes up and you sell the stock. If you select a stock that offers a quarterly or annual dividend, or payout based on the company's profits, you can also receive a dividend for each share of your stock if the company does well.

You can either invest in specific companies or invest in a fund of stocks. This is a way to spread out your investment over many stocks in order to safeguard your money from any one company not performing well. These funds can be broken down by their investment strategy. Here are some of the most common categories and sub-categories:

Index funds - In an index fund, the manager sets up his portfolio to mirror a market index — such as Standard & Poor's (S&P) 500-stock index — rather than actively picking which stocks to purchase. It is surprising, but true, that index funds often beat the majority of competitors among actively managed funds. One reason: few actively managed funds can consistently outperform the market by enough to cover the cost of their generally higher expenses.

Growth funds - These invest in the stock of companies whose profits are growing at a rapid pace. Such stocks typically rise more quickly than the overall market — and fall faster if they don't live up to investors' expectations.

Value funds - Value-oriented fund managers buy companies that appear to be cheap, relative to their earnings. In many cases, these are mature companies that send some of their earnings back to their shareholders in the form of dividends. Funds that specifically target such income-producing investments are often called equity-income or growth-and-income funds.

Growth-and-income, equity-income, and balanced funds - Growth-and-income funds concentrate more than the other two on growth, so they generally have the lowest yields. Balanced funds strive to keep anywhere from 50 to 60% of their holdings in stocks and the rest in interest-paying securities such as bonds and convertibles, giving them the highest yields. In the middle is the equity-income class.

Sector and specialty funds - Rather than diversifying their holdings, sector and specialty funds concentrate their assets in a particular sector, such as technology or health care. There's nothing wrong with that approach, as long as you remember that one year's top sector could crash the following year.

International - Funds that invest outside the U.S. come in three basic flavors. The first, international funds, typically buy stocks in larger companies from relatively stable regions like Europe and the Pacific Rim. Global funds do likewise, but they can also invest heavily in the United States. Emerging market funds invest in riskier regions, like Latin America, Eastern Europe and Asia.

As anyone knows, the stock market can be volatile. We will go into more detail concerning stocks in our next chapter. We will examine the history of the stock market return since the inception of the Dow Jones, S&P and

NASDAQ indexes.

Bonds

A bond is a debt investment in which an investor loans money to an entity (typically corporate, or governmental) which borrows the funds for a defined period of time at a variable or fixed interest rate. Companies, municipalities, states and sovereign governments use bonds to raise money and finance a variety of projects and activities. Owners of bonds are debtholders, or creditors of the issuer.

When companies or other entities need to raise money to finance new projects, maintain ongoing operations, or refinance existing other debts, they may issue bonds directly to investors instead of obtaining loans from a bank. The issuer produces a bond that contractually states the interest rate that will be paid and the time at which the loaned funds must be returned.

Typically bonds are issued for 2 to 30 years' maturity. The general movement in the interest rate causes the volatility in the price of the bonds.

Real Estate

Real estate is property comprised of land and the buildings on it as well as the natural resources of the land. Although the media often refers to the "real estate market" from the perspective of residential living, real estate can be grouped into three broad categories based on its use: residential, commercial and industrial. Examples of residential real estate include undeveloped land, houses, condominiums and townhomes. Commercial real estate consists of office buildings, warehouses and retail store buildings. Industrial real estate is typically factories, mines and farms.

For an investment or home purchase, real estate is the one investment that you can leverage to get more than what your money would normally buy. Say you wanted to buy a house worth $1,000,000. With good credit, you can obtain a mortgage for this building by putting $200,000 down and having a bank lend you the balance. If the property were to increase in value 10%, it would be worth $100,000 more than when you purchased it, giving you a 50% return on your $200,000 down payment (minus your interest payments and other related expenses).

Cash

Cash in its physical form is known as money. Cash usually includes bank accounts and marketable securities, such as government bonds and banker's acceptances. Although cash typically refers to money in hand, the term can also be used to indicate money in banking accounts, checks or any other form of currency that is easily accessible and can be quickly turned into physical cash without losing any of the principle.

Commodities

A commodity is a basic good used in commerce that is interchangeable with other commodities of the same type. Commodities are most often used as inputs in the production of other goods or services. The quality of a given commodity may differ slightly, but it is essentially uniform across producers.

Some traditional examples of commodities include grains, gold, beef, oil and natural gas. More recently, the definition has expanded to include financial products such as foreign currencies and indexes. Technological advances have also led to new types of commodities being exchanged in the marketplace, such as cell phone minutes and bandwidth. The sale and purchase of commodities is usually carried out through futures contracts on exchanges that standardize the quantity and minimum quality of the commodity being traded.

Cash-Value Life Insurance

This is the type of life insurance policy that pays out upon the policyholder's death, and also accumulates value during the policyholder's lifetime. The policyholder can use the cash value or account value as a tax-sheltered investment (the interest and earnings on the policy are tax-deferred and can be taken out tax-free), as a fund from which to pay for retirement, fund college expenses, purchase a house or for any other purpose, or they can pass the benefits to their heirs. Whole life, variable life and universal life are all types of cash-value life insurance. Cash-value insurance is also known as permanent life insurance because it provides coverage for the policyholder's entire life.

Comparison of Various Asset Classes:

Following is the comparison of six main asset classes by the average long term return, risk category, liquidity and tax-efficient yield:

Asset Class	Long Term Return	Risk	Liquidity	Taxable or Tax-free
Stocks	7%	Very High	Very Low	Taxable
Bonds	4%	Low	Medium	Taxable

Asset Class	Long Term Return	Risk	Liquidity	Taxable or Tax-free
Real Estate	6%	High	Very Low	Taxable
Cash	2%	No Risk	Very High	Taxable
Commodities	6%	Very High	Very Low	Taxable
Whole Life Insurance	4.5%	Low	Medium	Tax-free
S&P Index Universal Life Insurance	6.86%	Low	Medium	Tax-free

Asset Allocation by Ray Dalio

Ray Dalio is the founder of the world's biggest hedge fund firm, Bridgewater Associates, which managed $160 billion in assets. He is the 79th richest man in the world as of January 2019, according to Bloomberg. He has been investing since he was 12 years old when he bought $300 of Northeast Airline stock. He tripled his investment when the airline merged with another company.

Ray is famous for his "All Weather Portfolio" investment philosophy and hedge fund, one of the largest hedge funds in the world. He refined this concept as a way to balance out the different pros and cons of each type of investment. This "All Weather Portfolio" has produced around 10%

return with average loss of just under 2%, and the worst was just under 4%. He explains that you need 30% of your investment portfolio in stocks (for instance, the S&P 500 or other indexes for further diversification in this basket). Another necessary component is long-term government bonds. He suggests a breakdown of 15% in intermediate term bonds (7 to 10 years in maturity) and 40% in long-term bonds (20 to 25 in maturity). The stability of the bonds counters the volatility of the stocks.

He wants you to round out the portfolio with 7.5% in gold and 7.5% in commodities. As he says, "You need to have a piece of that portfolio that will do well with accelerated inflation so you would want a percentage in gold and commodities. These have high volatility because there are environments where rapid inflation can hurt both stocks and bonds."

Lastly, you have to actively keep balancing the portfolio. This means that when one segment does well, you must sell a portion of it and reallocate its proceeds back to the original allocation. This should be done at least annually and if done properly can actually increase the tax efficiency of the investments.

While I agree wholeheartedly with Mr. Dalio's philosophy and asset allocation, my only enhancement would be to use general account-based cash value life insurance as an alternative to long-term bond allocation. It creates tax-efficiency, while adding death benefits into the equation. As we will see, there are significant tax savings and other aspects of life insurance that can-round out a solid investment plan.

Second Factor Affecting Return: Taxation of Investments

Understanding taxation of your investments is crucial to maximizing returns. Due to the complexities of both investing and U.S. tax laws, many investors don't understand how to manage their portfolio to minimize their tax burden. We'll talk further about this in the twelfth chapter, but here we are simply discussing the tax efficiency during the accumulation phase of your money.

Tax efficiency is a measure of how much of an investment's return is left over after taxes. The more that an investment relies on investment income rather than a change in its price to generate a return, the less tax-efficient it is to the investor. Different asset classes like stocks and bonds are taxed differently in the United States and often play much different roles in the investor's portfolio. Historically, investors purchased bonds to provide an income stream for their portfolios, and bonds have generally enjoyed lower volatility or risk than stocks. The interest income from most bonds is taxable (municipal bonds which are a tax-efficient vehicle at the Federal tax level are an exception) and, therefore, are tax-inefficient to the investor in a higher tax bracket. Stocks are often purchased to provide a portfolio with growth or gains in their capital, as well as a current income stream from dividends.

Tax-efficiency is within reach of most investors. If you want to keep more of your investment earnings and stay out of a higher tax bracket, choose investments that offer the lowest tax burdens relative to their interest income or dividend income. You may also want to consider your opportunities for investing tax-free. Cash Value life insurance and Annuities enjoy special tax advantages and should be part of your investment portfolio. Given the market's persistent volatility, your decisions regarding tax-efficient investing may spell the difference between reaching your financial goals and falling short.

Third Factor Affecting Return: Expenses of Investments

This is a complex topic. There are fees in any type of investment. Some methods are very clear-cut in their fees. For instance, if you are buying property, many of the fees are laid out for you. Now if you are obtaining a mortgage, some of the bank fees are spelled out and some are part of the interest you pay back to the bank. The same thing is true on something simple like a CD. The bank is certainly charging you, but it is hidden by the interest that they are not paying you.

In just about every type of investment mentioned in this chapter, there are various charges that are either spelled out or hidden. Sometimes you pay them upfront and in other instances, they come off the earnings. There could be an annual fee. In fact, there seems to be as many types of fees as there are investments, so look over your paperwork carefully, or have an expert nearby who can help.

These are questions you need to ask if you are about to put your money into something. Some of the fees can get quite expensive and have a bearing on what you actually make on that investment. Say you put $10,000 into a stock fund and your first year return was 8% ($800). If that particular fund had various fees associated with it that added up to $200, then you only end up with $600. If you are in the 37% tax bracket, there goes another $222. You are now down to a $378 net return. (By the way, if anyone is showing you what an investment earns, they rarely, if ever, factor in the expenses and the taxes.)

We will get into a bit more of the specific taxes and expenses for the various investment categories, but that is something that you need to closely monitor. An investment might look good on paper, but your earnings could be eroded before you even get to spend them.

As we start talking about the specifics of each investment, please keep in mind everything we have already covered. Having that perspective will help you see how each one fits into the big picture. Since you want to be invested in each category to some degree, it is good to be familiar with their highlights.

You probably realize at this point that investing your money is not as easy as picking a bank or a stock or a mutual fund. You might have thought that once you did that, you only needed to give it a quick review every now and then. The people that think like that are the ones who have paid the government more in taxes than they should have and did not have, quite as big of a nest egg at retirement as they could have.

Summary

As you begin to put a strategy together, remember these key points:

- Don't lump your money into ONE basket,
- Pick the right asset classes for you,
- Regularly rebalance the portfolio,
- Choose indexed funds for your stock, gold and commodities allocation,
- Choose investment grade government and municipal bonds, cash rich whole life/fixed annuity for your fixed income allocation.

Your investment portfolio is not meant to be stagnant. Just as you keep up on the latest innovations for whatever business you are in, you need to do the same with your money. You don't need to be an expert; you can hire professional help. However, you should know what your money is doing, and be aware of new methods or plans that can complement your portfolio.

CHAPTER 6

Know the Real Return on Stocks

"Unless you can watch your stock holding decline by 50% without becoming panic-stricken, you should not be in the stock market."

Warren Buffett

In the previous chapter, you saw an overview of stocks. In its simplest form, a stock represents ownership in a company. The more shares you own, the greater your equity in that particular business. You can make money on a stock based on its appreciation and the amount of a dividend the stock pays out to its holder. Conversely, there may be no dividends and a stock can drop in value below what you paid for it.

The concept of stock ownership goes back to the Roman Empire. Just as the government does now, the Romans contracted their services out to private companies. Somebody had to make the swords and shields! These government contractors were similar to modern corporations in a couple of aspects. They issued shares called *partes* for large investors and *particulae,* which were small shares that acted like today's over-the-counter shares. Apparently, the Romans experienced the same highs and lows that today's stock market experiences. The Roman orator Cicero even spoke about "shares that had a very high price at that time."

Over the centuries, this concept went through evolution and refinement, which still goes on today. In fact, we will see how some relatively new tweaks to the stock market turned it into the behemoth we have now.

As shown earlier, there are different types of stocks. This might be one of the more complicated investments we have. Without clear guidance or putting the time in to learn about stocks, it is easy to make a wrong decision. Very often, you might think you are looking at two stocks that seem similar, but you are actually comparing apples and oranges. In general, remember that shares represent a fraction of ownership in a business. A business may declare different types (or classes) of shares, each having distinctive ownership rules, privileges, or share values. Ownership of shares may be documented by issuance of a stock certificate. A stock certificate is a legal document that specifies the amount of shares owned by the shareholder, and other details of the shares.

Stock typically takes the form of shares that are either common stock or preferred stock. Common stock typically carries voting rights exercised in corporate decisions. Preferred stock does not carry such voting rights, but the holder is legally entitled to receive a certain level of dividend payments before any dividends can be issued to other shareholders. "Convertible preferred stock" is preferred stock that includes an option for the holder to convert the preferred shares into a fixed number of common shares, usually any time after a predetermined date.

That is the basic framework of stocks. You can purchase stocks as individual shares in a particular company, or you can buy shares in a fund. A stock fund consists of a number of individual stocks. The concept behind them is that you are spreading your money out over a variety of companies, so that no one poorly performing stock can flush all of your money down the drain. It is another example of "not putting all of your eggs in one basket." Any dividends or money made by selling stocks in the fund goes back into the fund and is used to pay shareholders of the fund. Of course, if the fund experiences an overall loss, the shareholders share in that too.

Many times, these funds have a theme. A "tech fund" specializes in technology stocks. You can have a fund investing in stocks that are more conservative, while a "rapid growth" fund goes after something a little more speculative. You can have funds that are full of purely domestic stocks and international funds that invest overseas. Like almost everything having to do with stocks, you have to look carefully at the makeup of a fund you are thinking about investing in.

The appeal of the stock market is that it is the major financial investment talked about the most. The media uses it as a barometer of how the economy is doing. Investment advisors tout its overall growth and sustainability as a place to put your money. When compared to what banks offer in interest these days, it seems like a no brainer to jump into the stock market where "real money" can be made.

To help explain some of the stock market's history, it is good to have impartial statistics. MeasuringWorth.com is a nonprofit with two missions. The first is to make available to the public the highest quality and most reliable historical data on important economic aggregates, with particular emphasis on nominal (current-price) measures, as well as real (constant-price) measures. The second is to provide carefully designed contrasts (using these data) that explain the many issues involved in making value comparisons over time. The advisors of MeasuringWorth.com represent some of the finest universities of the United States and Great Britain, such as Harvard, Stanford, Oxford, Northwestern, etc. The nonprofit is not connected to any institution and as their website describes, it "strives to give arbitrary service for calculating relative worth over time."

First, we are going to look at historical market data from them. The annual growth rate of the "Dow Jones Industrial Average" (DJIA) between its inception on February 16, 1885 and February 28, 2019, is 5.14%. The growth rate of the "S&P 500" since its inception on March 4, 1957 to February 28, 2019, is 6.92%. The growth rate of the "NASDAQ" since its inception on February 5, 1971 until February 28, 2019 is 9.42%.

Historic Stock Market Returns

From	To	DIJA	S & P 500	NASDAQ
2/16/1885	02/28/2019	5.14%	N/A	N/A
12/30/1950	12/30/1960	10.09%	N/A	N/A
12/30/1960	12/30/1970	3.17%	4.73%	N/A
12/30/1970	12/30/1980	1.35%	3.90%	7.28%
12/30/1980	12/31/1990	10.59%	9.33%	6.43%
12/30/1990	01/02/2001	14.99%	14.57%	19.93%
12/30/2000	12/31/2010	0.70%	-0.48%	0.71%
12/31/2010	02/28/2019	10.40%	10.25%	13.68%

1940 - 1950

At one time, the stock market did grow along the lines of the American economy. The period from 1941 to 1950 encompasses World War II and the years immediately after. For the first half of the decade, America was on a war footing and most of the country was in the business of fueling the war machine. The government was the primary buyer of goods and many companies retooled to support the effort. General Motors made tanks, Ford made airplanes, etc. The latter part of the decade was a "war hangover" as companies switched back to domestic production and had to deal with an influx of workers returning to the home front. During this decade, the average return on stocks was 4.34%.

1950 – 1960

The fifties were an economic boom in the United States. Not only did the country have plenty of consumers making good wages to buy goods, the country was supplying many products to the world. The devastation of Europe and other parts of the globe made it difficult for companies in those countries get up to speed again. While they were struggling, America picked up the slack. If you look at the average growth of 10% in the stock market during this time, American companies were strong, as was the overall economy.

1960 - 1970

In the sixties, hiccups began to occur. American companies had international competition for many products. The country had internal struggles with civil rights and the Vietnam War. It is difficult to keep up any ten-year surge such as the one experienced in the 1950's. If you throw all of that in the mix, companies began to slow down and not grow as rapidly. Internal turmoil in the country resulted in more conservative investment practices. The stock market reflects this in its average 3 to 4% growth rate that occurred during this decade.

1970 - 1980

If there were hiccups in the 60's, then the patient was almost dead in the 70's. Inflation was very high, as was unemployment, and there was a lack of confidence in the economy. This was the decade of Watergate, a president resigning in disgrace, and long lines of cars waiting for gasoline. It seems like the country was about to collapse under its own weight. Growth in the stock market or almost anything else was almost nonexistent during that time. You can see this reduction of growth was on average only 2 to 4% during the 1970's, representing the lowest in the last 60 years of the 20th century.

Ironically, this was the last decade where the stock market coincided closely with how the companies were actually performing financially. It is important to note that up to the 1980's, the leading investors in the stock market were very wealthy individuals and huge institutional investors. This would soon change.

1980 – Today

The best and the brightest tried to figure out how to infuse the stock market with a huge influx of cash. When you get past institutional investors and the few people who had more money than they knew what to do with, all that was left were the common folk. They never really had any means or way to get into the stock market. This was the target group that those running the markets wanted.

They laid the groundwork in 1974 with the enactment of the Employee Retirement Income Security Act (ERISA). Taxpayers could contribute up to fifteen percent of their annual income or $1,500, whichever is less, each year and reduce their taxable income by the amount of their contributions. These contributions could be invested in a special United States bond paying 6% interest that would begin paying out when the contributor reached the age of 59½. Originally, it was only available to workers that were not covered by a qualified employment-based retirement plan.

In 1981, the Economic Recovery Tax Act (ERTA) allowed all working taxpayers under the age of 70½ to contribute to an IRA, regardless of their coverage under a qualified plan. The IRS also raised the maximum annual contribution to $2,000 and allowed participants to contribute $250 on behalf of a nonworking spouse. This was the law that opened the floodgates for the average person into the stock market. As modifications to the law continued to come down the road, they allowed different financial vehicles to be established that met the criteria of the law, but allowed investment in stocks. For the most part, this was done through investing in mutual stock funds and a huge influx of cash poured into the stock market.

Companies established how many shares of stocks they could issue. They can split stocks as time goes on, or issue more for a specific reason, but it isn't like the stock of a company was an infinite number. Therefore, when you have a great deal of money to purchase stocks, and only so much stock is available, the law of supply and demand kicks in. When demand outweighs supply, prices go up. Stock prices did just that, to an altitude never seen before.

This completed the transition from the stock market being a somewhat accurate barometer of the corporate strength of the nation's companies to becoming a manufactured entity. Its gains and losses had more to do with the proliferation of money available to invest in the stock market, rather than the performance of the companies on the stock exchange. You often hear financial and political commentators say there is a disconnect between Wall Street and Main Street (meaning how well the stock market is doing compared to the average American's income.) This is where that disconnect began.

Other man-made factors affected stocks. Income tax rates saw their biggest cut ever, especially at the high end of the income scale. People with large incomes had even more money to invest, and the stock market was one of their targets. Financial companies were coming up with products as fast as they could to feed the public's thirst for the stock market. This was like throwing wood on an already out-of-control fire. The money going through the stock market increased its size and value dramatically. The thing is, even though the economy was getting a little better as compared to the 1970's, it was nowhere near what was the actual growth of the stock market.

This artificial stock market boom lasted for a good twenty years. It is arguably one of the longest periods of prosperity in the stock market history. However, any resemblance to how Wall Street was doing compared to the rest of the country was purely coincidental. Some industries like technology boomed, but other mainstays of the American economy such as automobile manufacturers suffered. As you can see from the chart, the 80's and 90's had unprecedented growth.

It came to a grinding halt during the first decade of the 21st century. America had the tragedy of 9/11, wars in Iraq and Afghanistan, and a sense of uncertainty throughout all facets of the country. Then the recession of 2008 hit, and people discovered that many of our financial institutions were built on on a foundation of sand. The government had to bail out the same large corporations that used to look at them in disdain whenever they tried to impose government regulations. The world was upside down.

The government's rescue of the economy helped Wall Street to make up what it lost and to gain ground. For instance, the Federal Reserve basically allowed large institutions to borrow money for free as a way to get the economic machine moving again. Many companies took advantage of miniscule interest rates, and took the money they borrowed to put into the stock market. Again, the stock market took advantage of a new infusion of cash to grow.

Now and in the future, the stock market is its own entity with almost no bearing on the actual strength of its underlying companies. If you listen to many companies today, their mission is not necessarily putting out the best product or providing the best service. Companies are shooting for increasing profits, but more often than not, a company primariy wants to keep their stockholders happy. For a CEO, not realizing a decent dividend in a year may cost him or her their job. This focus plays havoc with the management of companies.

While the stock market has had its booming years in recent history, remember what we talked about in an earlier chapter about looking at numbers. They can be skewed to fit almost any picture that a person wants to make, if you don't know the full story.

Overall, the stock market is a good hedge against inflation over the long haul, but not by any large margin. It should certainly be a part of an investment portfolio, but care must be given to the percentage of money you want to put into stocks. Then you have to decide what kind of stocks you are going to buy with that set amount of money.

The stock market's allure has been the undoing of many investors. It is a game that is played for huge stakes. Only a little over a decade ago, many people lost their investments in the stock market when things went belly up in 2008. While the ship righted itself, it wasn't on its own, and there are no guarantees that it will do so again if things go south.

Summary

Stocks are the highest performing asset class compare to any other asset classes over the long term and deserve a place in most people's investment portfolios. The biggest learning from this chapter is to expect reasonable rate of returns from stocks, and limit the allocation to balance the two economic powers – the power of short fluctuating return and the power of actuarial science. You will learn more about this in Chapter Twelve and Chapter Fourteen. The asset allocation model of Ray Dalio's "All Weather Portfolio" is also a great guiding principle for the right allocation in stocks as we discussed in the previous chapter.

The dynamics of the stock market have changed dramatically over the past eighty years. The performance of a stock used to closely mirror the success (or difficulties) of its company. That is not necessarily the case these days. Huge amounts of money are invested in stocks every day. While a company's performance will still affect its stock, other issues like taxes, money supply, interest rates, the international situation, and a host of other factors all have a bearing on the market. Investing in stocks always had the potential of volatility, but that is truer now than ever before.

Keep in mind, in the second decade of this century, the stock market has had incredible highs as it constantly breaks records after bottoming out in 2008, when it almost took down some very large companies and financial institutions. Some investors made a lot of money in this time, but many lost a lot, too. The thing that surprises many people is that with all the hoopla surrounding the stock market, the average investor will only realize a 7% return on the money they put into stocks. You may hear of people making a "killing" in the stock market, but they are few and far between and that is their life's work. Others have lost almost everything on the turn of a bad stock.

That is something to keep in mind with all but the most conservative investments: there are no guarantees. That should be your mantra as you explore the stock market, and other investments for that matter. Your goal is to create wealth, not end up breaking even...or worse.

CHAPTER 7

The Bond Market

"Rule number one: Don't lose money.
Rule number two: Don't forget rule number one."

Warren Buffett

A bond is a financial security in which the issuer of the bond is taking the bondholder's money with a promise to pay it back with interest. Sometimes referred to as a debt security, the terms of the bond dictate when and how much the issuer pays back to the holder of the bond. Unlike stocks, which have no clear timetable and rate of return, bonds clearly state how much interest the issuer will pay and when. Monthly, semiannually, or annually are the usual timeframes.

There is also a maturity date fixed to the bond. This date is when the issuer will also pay back the original principal paid for the bond. A very simple example is that you purchase a $50,000 bond with a ten-year maturity date and an interest rate of 3% payable annually. Every year you will receive $1500 as an interest payment, and you will get back your $50,000 investment after ten years.

Bonds allow the issuer to bring in a great deal of money when initially selling the bonds. They can then use that cash for whatever purpose they issued the bonds for. We will go into more detail on this a little farther in the chapter, but there are three main issuers of bonds:

- Government – sold by a national government where income from bonds helps finance current expenditures.

- Municipal – sold by states and local municipalities who earmark the funds raised by the bonds to fund a particular project – usually infrastructure related.

- Corporate – as the name implies, issued by companies to fund expansion, research, mergers & acquisitions, etc.

Once you buy a bond, you can transfer it into the secondary market where it can be bought and sold, similar to a stock. In other words, a bondholder does not necessarily have to hang on to a bond until its maturity date. It can be sold ahead of time. Even though bonds are thought of as a stable investment, they can have a high volatility based on the movement in general interest rates.

As you can see, if you buy a bond you are basically receiving an IOU from the issuer. You are the lender, and the issuer is the borrower. Before the advent of electronic transactions, physical bonds were issued with coupons attached that the bondholder would turn in for their interest payments. For that reason, you will often hear the interest rate referred to as the coupon rate. That amount is what you the lender receives as payment for the use of your money.

Maturity Date

Before we explore the varieties of bonds available on the market for investing, let's look at some terminology that is important to know. I have already alluded to the maturity date. This is when the issuer has to pay the bondholder the face value of the bond. Let's say it is the $50,000 bond in the earlier example. The bondholder is due that fifty grand on the maturity date. The issuer has no further obligation to the bondholder after the maturity date as long as it made all payments on the bond.

Rating of Bonds

Potential investors look at the credit rating of a bond as a leading indicator of the amount of risk involved with investing in it. The higher the credit rating, the more secure the investment. Credit rating agencies such as Moody's and Standard & Poor's use letter designations, which characterizes the soundness of a bond. Moody's assigns bond ratings of Aaa, Aa, A, Baa, Ba, B, Caa, Ca, and C. Standard & Poor's ratings are similar: AAA, AA, A, BBB, BB, B, CCC, CC, C, and D.

Investment grade (or IG) bonds have a credit rating of BBB or higher by Standard & Poor's or Baa3 or higher by Moody's. In the judgement of the rating agency, these bonds are likely to meet their payment obligations.

The ratings also help determine the amount of interest an issuer needs to pay on their bonds. The issuers' borrowing costs are going to be greatly affected depending on if the rating agencies rate them as investment-grade or speculative-grade. Bonds that are not rated as investment-grade bonds are known as high-yield bonds or more derisively as "junk bonds."

Type of Bonds

Government Bonds

A national government issues this type of bond. In general, the government promises to pay periodic interest payments on the bond and to repay the face value on the maturity date. Government bonds are usually issued in the country's own currency. United States bonds are issued in dollars, of course, and they are backed by the "full faith and credit" of the United States government.

The Netherlands issued the first general government bonds in 1517. Issued by the city of Amsterdam, the average interest rate at that time fluctuated around 20%. Britain issued the first national government bond through the Bank of England in 1694 to raise money to finance a war against France. Since that time, the issuing of bonds has become standard practice for many countries. It has progressed from a way to pay for a war to financing the everyday operations of the government.

Federal Government bonds are theoretically "risk-free" since the government can raise taxes or create additional currency to meet its debt obligations. Rarely does a country default on its bond obligations, though it has happened. Russia did this back in 1998 when it was going through its "ruble crisis." Those instances are very rare. Governments are also rated on their ability to pay back their debts. If you are looking at the bonds of other countries, you need to pay attention to that factor.

If you are considering investing in United States Treasury securities, there are three categories of bond maturities:

- Short term (bills): maturities between one and five years. (Financial instruments with maturities less than one year are called Money Market Instruments.)

- Medium term (notes): maturities between six and twelve years.

- Long term (bonds): maturities greater than twelve years.

Following the 10 year US treasury rate by the year:

Year	Rate
01/01/1871	5.32%
01/01/1901	3.10%
01/01/1925	3.86%
01/01/1951	2.57%
01/01/1961	3.84%
01/01/1971	6.24%
01/01/1981	12.57%
01/01/1991	8.09%
01/01/2001	5.16%

Year	Rate
01/01/2011	3.39%
01/01/2015	1.88%

Municipal Bonds

This is a bond issued by a local government or territory, or their agencies. The United States has the largest market of such securities in the world. Issuers of municipal bonds can be states, cities, counties, redevelopment agencies, special-purpose districts, school districts, public utility districts, publicly owned airports and seaports, and any other governmental entity (or group of governments) at or below the state level.

Many countries in the world also issue municipal bonds, sometimes called local authority bonds. The main characteristic of this type of bond is that a lower level of government than the national government issues the bond. The U.S. municipal bond market is unique for its size, liquidity, legal and tax structure, and bankruptcy protection afforded by the U.S. Constitution.

In America, interest income received by holders of these bonds does not have to be reported for federal income tax purposes under Section 103 of the Internal Revenue Code. It may also be exempt from state income tax depending on the applicable state income tax laws and the type of municipal bonds. Usually, the market factors in the tax advantages of municipal bonds, and the return will be lower than comparable taxable bonds.

An investor is free to trade many municipal bonds once they are purchased. Professional traders regularly trade and re-trade the same bonds several times a week. Smaller retail investors purchase a large proportion of municipal bonds as compared to other sectors of the U.S. securities markets.

Municipal securities consist of both short-term issues, often called notes since they typically mature in one year or less, and long-term issues. These get the designation of "bonds" since they mature in a year or more. The short-term notes are issued for a variety of reasons. It enables a government to get money now in anticipation of future revenues such as taxes, state or federal aid payments, and future bond issuances. They can cover cash flow issues, meet sudden deficits, and raise immediate capital for projects until long-term financing is finalized.

Bonds usually finance capital infrastructure projects needed over the long term. These projects vary greatly, but can include schools, streets and highways, bridges, hospitals, public housing, sewer, water systems, power utilities, and various public projects.

There are two types of municipal bonds. The general obligation bonds are secured by the full faith and credit of the issuer and usually supported by either the issuer's unlimited or limited taxing power. In many cases, voters have to approve general obligation bonds. Revenue bonds are backed by revenues from tolls, charges, or rents earned by the facility built with the proceeds of the bond issued. Public projects financed by revenue bonds include toll roads, bridges, airports, water and sewage treatment facilities, hospitals, and subsidized housing. Special authorities created for that particular purpose issue many of these bonds.

Most municipal notes and bonds are issued in minimum denominations of $5,000 or multiples of $5,000. Interest is either a fixed or a variable rate subjected to a cap known as the maximum legal limit. The issuer of a municipal bond receives a cash purchase price at the time of issuance in exchange for a promise to repay the purchasing investors or bondholders (if the purchaser sold the bond) over time. Repayment periods can be as short as a few months (although this is very rare) to 20, 30, or 40 years.

Corporate Bonds

Corporations issue corporate bonds in order to raise capital for a variety of reasons. It can be for ongoing operations or to expand business. The term "bond" usually applies to securities with maturity of at least one year. Corporate debt instruments with maturity shorter than a year are known as commercial paper.

There are two types of corporate bonds. There are High Grade (also called Investment Grade) and High Yield (known as Non-Investment Grade, Speculative Grade, or Junk Bonds). The bond's credit rating determines their classification. Bonds rated AAA, AA, A, and BBB are High Grade, while bonds rated BB and below are High Yield. There are significant distinctions as different types of investors purchase both type of bonds. For example, many pension funds and insurance companies are prohibited from holding more than a token amount of High Yield bonds (by internal rules or government regulation.) The distinction between High Grade and High Yield is also common to most corporate bond markets.

The interest earned (coupon value) on corporate bonds is usually taxable income for the investor. It is tax deductible for the corporation paying it. Sometimes the coupon can be zero. When this happens, the zero-coupon bond is sold at a discount. For example, let's look at a $1000 face value bond sold for $800. The investor pays $800, but collects $1000 at maturity.

Some corporate bonds have an embedded call option that allows the issuer to redeem the debt before its maturity date. These are called callable bonds. Other bonds, known as convertible bonds, allow investors to convert the bond into equity, such as a common or preferred stock. They can also be secured or unsecured, senior or subordinated, and issued out of different parts of the company's capital structure. As you can see, there are many facets to corporate bonds.

Deferred Fixed Annuity - Like a Government Bond

Deferred annuities are classified by the method the insurance company uses to determine how interest is credited to the annuity contract. A fixed annuity is the simplest of deferred annuity, and generally offers the annuity owner a guaranteed interest rate for a certain period of time. Once the initial period ends, a new interest rate is established. The fact that fixed annuities have guaranteed principal and interest make them much like the government bond or a Certificates of Deposit (CD) that banks sell. Usually, a fixed annuity pays higher return than comparable government bonds and CDs with tax-deferred growth of the interest.

Bonds vs Stocks

While bonds and stocks are both securities, the main difference between the two is that a stockholder has an ownership stake in a company, whereas bondholders have a creditor stake in the company (in other words, they are lenders.) Being a creditor, bondholders have priority over stockholders. This means they will be repaid in advance of the stockholders, but will rank behind secured creditors if the company files for bankruptcy. Bonds also have a defined maturity term when they have to be redeemed, while stocks can usually be owned indefinitely.

Institutions such as central banks, sovereign wealth funds, pension funds, insurance companies, hedge funds, and banks buy and trade corporate bonds. Insurance companies and pension funds have liabilities that include fixed amounts payable on predetermined dates. They buy bonds to match their liabilities, as their policies, and sometimes the law dictates what they are allowed to purchase. Individuals who want to own bonds do so through bond funds. In the United States, households still hold nearly 10% of all outstanding bonds.

The volatility of bonds is lower than that of stocks. For this reason, bonds are considered a safer investment than stocks. Bonds are not subject to the day-to-day volatility of stocks. Their interest payments are sometimes higher than the general level of dividend payments of equities. Bonds are often liquid and it is easy for an institution to sell a large quantity of them without having too much effect on the price. That is not true of the equities market where buying and selling has a direct consequence on its price. For many investors, the general certainty of a fixed interest payment twice a year, and a fixed lump sum at maturity is attractive.

Corporate bonds are not completely risk-free. Fixed-rate bonds are subject to interest rate risk. This means that a bond's market price will decrease in value when the generally prevailing interest rates rise. Since the payments are fixed, a decrease in the market price of the bond means an increase in its yield. When the market interest rate rises, the market price of bonds will fall, reflecting an investor's ability to get a higher interest rate on their money elsewhere.

Bonds are also subject to various other risks, such as call and prepayment risk, credit risk, reinvestment risk, liquidity risk, event risk, exchange rate risk, volatility risk, inflation risk, sovereign risk, and yield curve risk. These are all terms to become familiar with if you are going to invest heavily in the bond market. Some of these will only affect certain classes of investors.

Mutual funds that hold corporate bonds are affected by the price changes in bonds. If the value of the bonds in their trading portfolio falls, the value of the portfolio also falls. This can hurt professional investors such as banks, insurance companies, pension funds and asset managers.

Bond prices can change if the credit rating of the issuer is upgraded or downgraded. An unanticipated downgrade will cause the market price of the bond to fall. As with interest rate risk, this risk does not affect the bond's interest payments (provided the issuer does not actually default), but puts at risk the market price, which affects mutual funds holding these bonds and holders of individual bonds who may have to sell them.

A company's bondholders could lose some or all of their money if the company goes bankrupt. As already discussed, the laws of many countries (including the United States) allow bondholders to receive the proceeds of the sale of the assets of a liquidated company ahead of some other creditors. Bank lenders, deposit holders, and trade creditors may take precedence. There is no guarantee of how much money will remain to repay bondholders.

As an example, WorldCom, a giant telecommunications company, went bankrupt in 2004. The company's bondholders received 35.7 cents on the dollar. This was certainly not close to the entire value, but it was more than the stockholders received.

Summary

Bonds are an investment that have more stability than stocks. As a "fixed-income" security, the rate of return is fixed, and there are no mysteries about what an investor will receive by purchasing bonds. However, as this chapter briefly showed, there are still many variables to take into account when investing in bonds or bond funds.

With bonds, as with all investments, do your homework well on the subject and do not be afraid to seek advice and help from an expert. You need to have the best information possible when deciding if you want to invest in government, municipal, or corporate bonds – or some combination of all three. The broad view of bonds is that they are a good investment and should be part of your portfolio in some fashion. Each investor is different in deciding which ones will work best for them.

CHAPTER 8

The Complex World of Commodities

"Commodities tend to zig when the equity markets zag."

Jim Rogers

Commodity is a term used for an economic good or service that is interchangeable with other commodities of the same type. This means that the quality of a given commodity may differ slightly, but it is essentially uniform across producers. Commodities are the raw resources that go into other products. Examples include wheat, iron, pork, gold, oil and oranges. If you saw the comedy classic movie "Trading Places" with Eddie Murphy, you understand a little bit about the dynamics of the commodities world.

The demand and price for a commodity is very close to being the same across all markets. That is because oil is oil, no matter where the well is. While there are different grades of oil, the same grades are almost identical wherever they come out of the ground. This differs from something manufactured, like a laptop. A product like this differs from one company to another and has so many different design possibilities that they all vary in price. The demand for one type of laptop may be greater than another.

A commodity good has its price determined as a function of its market as a whole. Well-established physical commodities have actively traded markets. As a rule of thumb, soft commodities are agricultural goods such as wheat, coffee, cocoa and sugar. Hard commodities are extracted through mining like copper and silver. In addition, there are also energy commodities, which include electricity, gas, coal and oil. Electricity is a little different from the others since it has the characteristic that it is usually not economical to store, so it is consumed as soon as it is produced.

You can invest in commodities just as you do stocks and bonds. Like those other investments, commodities have their own markets. Investors access about 50 major commodity markets worldwide. Futures contracts are the oldest way of investing in commodities. You are purchasing a certain item like lemons or iron at a certain price. It depends on the market for that item on whether the price goes up or down.

Commodities are the oldest form of marketing in civilization. Historians believe that commodity-based money and commodity markets originated in Sumer between 4500 BC and 4000 BC. Sumerians first used clay tokens sealed in a clay vessel, then clay writing tablets to represent the amount for example, the number of sheep to be delivered. These promises of time and date of delivery resemble futures contracts. Early civilizations used pigs, rare seashells, or other items as commodity money. Since that time, traders have sought ways to simplify and standardize trade contracts.

Two early commodities that still demand attention today are gold and silver. In the beginning, people valued them for their beauty and intrinsic worth and their association with royalty. Soon early civilizations used them for the trading and exchanging of goods or as payment for labor. Specific measurements of gold and silver became money. The scarcity, unique density, and the way they could be easily melted, shaped, and measured made gold and silver natural trading assets.

The first stock exchange was actually a commodities market. The Amsterdam Stock Exchange, founded in 1602, began as a market for the exchange of commodities. Early trading on the Amsterdam Stock Exchange often involved the use of very sophisticated contracts, including short sales, forward contracts, and options. In 1864, the Chicago Board of Trade (CBOT) became the main marketplace for selling wheat, corn, cattle, and pigs in the United States. It has since taken on other commodities like rice, mill feeds, butter, eggs, Irish potatoes and soybeans.

Successful commodities markets require broad consensus on product variations to make each commodity acceptable for trading, such as the purity of gold in bullion. This allows someone in the United States to know that the gold bought from Germany, for example, is the expected quality being sold. In its basic form, when you buy a commodity, it is something that you can reach out and touch if you so desire.

Like stocks and bonds, commodities can also be part of a fund. You can buy a share of a fund, and its performance depends on how the commodities within the fund perform. Like every investment we have talked about, doing your homework or picking the brain of an expert in commodities is necessary to put yourself in the best position to have a successful investment.

To further get an idea of how commodities work, let's look at three commodities that receive a lot of publicity and are actively traded on the market.

Gold

Of all the precious metals in which to invest, gold is the most popular. Investors generally buy gold as a way of diversifying risk. Like any other market, gold is subject to speculation and volatility. Historically, gold has been an effective safe haven as an investment and a way to hedge against the failure of other investments.

Supply and demand drive the price for gold, as well as the demand created by speculation. Unlike most commodities, the act of saving gold plays a larger role in affecting its price than its consumption. Most of the gold ever mined still exists in accessible form. It tends to be in the form of bullion or jewelry, and thus has the potential to come back onto the gold market for the right price. There is a huge amount of gold stored and recycled above ground compared to annual mining of the commodity. The price of gold is mainly affected by changes in demand rather than changes in annual production. According to the World Gold Council, annual mine production of gold over the last few years has been close to 2,500 tons. About 2,000 tons goes into jewelry or industrial/dental production, and around 500 tons goes to retail investors and into traded gold funds.

The traditional way of investing in gold is buying gold bullion bars. In some countries, like Canada, Austria and Switzerland, you can easily buy or sell these at major banks. Alternatively, there are bullion dealers that provide the same service. Bars are available in various sizes and generally carry lower price premiums than gold bullion coins. However, larger bars carry an increased risk of forgery due to their less stringent appearance requirements. Efforts to combat gold bar counterfeiting include kinebars, which employ a unique holographic technology.

Gold coins are another common way of owning gold. Bullion coins are priced according to their weight, plus a small premium based on supply and demand. The price of gold coins that were used as money is dictated by supply and demand based on rarity and condition.

If you do not want to worry about physically handling and storing actual gold bars or coins, gold certificates allow gold investors to avoid the transfer and storage of physical gold. There are other risks and costs associated with certificates such as commissions, storage fees, and various types of credit risk.

The first paper banknotes were gold certificates. They were first issued in the 17th century when goldsmiths in England and the Netherlands used them for customers who kept deposits of gold bullion in their vaults. Two hundred years later, the United States issued gold certificates that could be exchanged for gold. The US government first authorized the use of the gold certificates in 1863. On April 5, 1933, the US Government restricted private gold ownership in the United States and therefore, the gold certificates stopped circulating as money (this restriction was reversed on January 1, 1975.) Nowadays, gold certificates are still issued by gold pool programs in Australia and the United States, as well as by banks in Germany, Switzerland and Vietnam.

Historically, there have been five series for determining the value of gold. They are the British Official Price from 1257, London Market Price from 1718, U.S. Official Price from 1786 and New York Market price from 1791. The following is the historical price of Gold from 1791 based on the New York Market:

Year	US$ Per Fine Ounce
1791	$5.32
1814	$20.10
1864	$42.03
1879	$20.67

Year	US$ Per Fine Ounce
1934	$34.94
1967	$35.00
1973	$97.81
1974	$159.74
1979	$307.50
1980	$612.56
1985	$317.66
1990	$384.93
1995	$385.50
2000	$280.00
2005	$446.00
2010	$1,227.00
2015	$1,170.00

Year	US$ Per Fine Ounce
March 25th, 2019	$1,321.70

Gold vs. Stocks

The performance of gold bullion is often compared to stocks as an investment vehicle. Gold is regarded by some as a "store of value" (without growth), whereas stocks are regarded as a "return on value" when you factor in the hope of a real price increase in the stock plus dividends. Stocks and bonds perform best in a stable political climate with strong property rights and little turmoil.

Since 1800, stocks have consistently gained value in comparison to gold, in part because of the stability of the American political system. One argument is that in the long-term, gold's high volatility means it doesn't hold its value when compared to stocks and bonds.

There have been times where the price of gold has shot up through the stratosphere. This tends to happen when the United States or the world is in a very uncertain state. It is at that point that there is almost a psychological need for an investor to have something he or she can physically hang on to. The thinking goes, "The markets may tumble out of control, but I will have my gold to fall back on."

As with any commodity — or investment for that matter — the key with gold is knowing when to invest so you can take advantage of its appreciation. Of course, the counterpoint to that is selling before the price tumbles and reallocating your investment resources elsewhere.

Oil

Investors can directly invest in oil as a commodity. There are several ways to approach this. One simple way for the average person to invest in oil is through stocks of oil drilling and service companies. Another direct method of owning oil is through the purchase of oil futures or oil futures options. Futures are highly volatile and involve a high degree of risk. Additionally, investing in futures may require the investor to do a lot of homework as well as invest a large amount of capital.

Investors can gain more direct exposure to the price of oil through an exchange-traded fund (ETF) or exchange-traded note (ETN), which typically invest in oil futures contracts rather than energy stocks. Because oil prices are largely uncorrelated to stock market returns or the direction of the U.S. dollar, these products follow the price of oil more closely than energy stocks and can serve as a hedge against a market downturn, and as a way to diversify your portfolio.

In addition, investors can gain indirect exposure to oil through the purchase of energy-sector ETFs, and energy-sector mutual funds. These energy-specific ETFs and mutual funds invest solely in the stocks of oil and oil services companies and come with lower risk.

The oil market is confusing to both professionals and the average investor alike. There are large price swings, sometimes on a daily basis. It is an industry that is constantly evolving and changing. If you look at simple supply and demand, you can see one reason prices seesaw radically. Countries like the United States actually have decreased their need for oil. Even with emerging economies having an increased requirement for it, the overall drop in demand lowers prices.

The supply side of oil used to be closely monitored by OPEC. This consortium of oil-producing countries banded together to regulate how much oil they pumped out and sold to the world. As other sources of oil outside of the OPEC nations became available, their power and influence dropped along with plummeting oil prices. As the alliance weakened, certain countries like Saudi Arabia pumped out more oil in order to maintain their level of income with the lower price per barrel. This further increased the supply of oil and contributed to even lower prices.

The volatility in investing in oil can be seen right here in the United States over the last decade. When fracking became an economic method for extracting oil from shale, areas of the country boomed with renewed economic vigor as the oil industry expanded to areas never used for oil production before. Towns sprang up around these areas with a call for workers to travel to remote parts of Texas or North Dakota. The amount of oil surged, as did profits. A few short years later, the areas are ghost towns and wells are closed as the price of oil dropped and made those operations cost prohibitive. They could very well open again when the price of oil goes up.

The oil industry is also affected by the political winds of the world. When there is the threat of war or some other major upheaval, the price of oil goes up. If war threatens an oil producing nation, the price goes up that much higher. The joke is that if a camel sneezes wrong in the Mideast, oil goes up!

Oil is also at the mercy of waves of speculation in the marketplace. Sometimes it seems like the laws of supply and demand are thrown out the window, given how much the investing dollar can affect prices. Many major institutional investors are involved in the oil markets, such as pension and endowment funds. They hold commodity-linked investments as part of a long-term asset-allocation strategy. Others, including Wall Street speculators, trade oil futures for very short periods of time to reap quick profits. Some observers attribute wide short-term swings in oil prices to these speculators.

Following is the West Texas Intermediate (WTI) or NYMEX crude oil prices per barrel beginning in 1946, according to macrotrends.net:

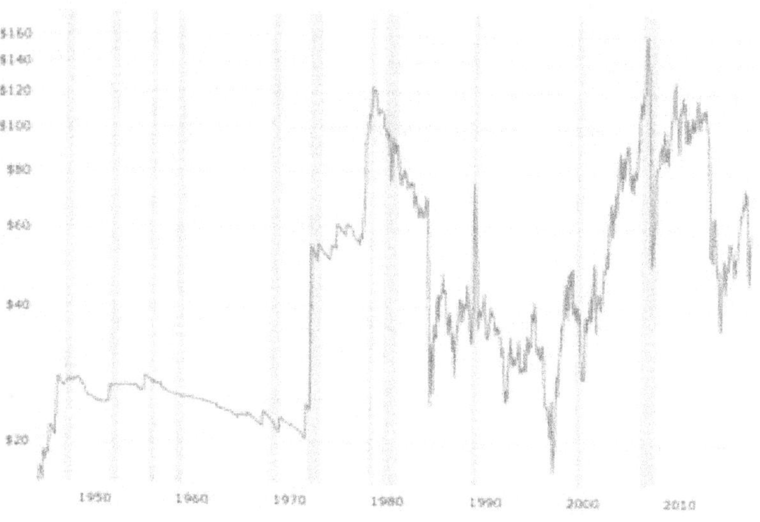

Currencies

As we learned in a preceding chapter, money is a commodity, and it is as actively traded as any grain or mineral. The foreign exchange market (Forex) is where currencies are traded. For speculators and investors, this market provides opportunities to take advantage of movements in exchange rates. There are different reasons why currency may be an attractive investment for certain investors.

Currency is one way to add balance to your portfolio. This is especially true if you are invested heavily in United States' equities. The way the currency market works is if you think that the dollar will drop in the future, you can buy one or more currencies that you think will rise. A difference to keep in mind between stocks and currencies is that stocks move independently of each other, while currencies move relative to each other. This means that when one currency is rising, another must be falling.

Another consideration is that the news which can cause currencies to rise and fall is available to everyone on a real-time basis. Since events that influence a country's economic health determine currency values, you can do your own research to judge what is going to affect any particular currency. You can select currencies based on how you perceive their relative values will change over time.

Something that currencies have in common with other commodities, as well as stocks, is their high volatility. If the value of your currencies rises against the dollar, you will profit. If your currencies fall relative to the dollar, you will lose money.

While the concept of how investing in currencies appears simple, there is substantial risk involved. You need to have an understanding of international relations and economics to help figure out how the ramifications of crucial world events will affect currency values. In today's world, significant events can happen at a moment's notice, which can bring a huge measure of volatility to short-term currency values.

To minimize your risk, it helps to spread your investments as you would with equities. Choose countries that you will follow closely. It is best to invest in a currency whose countries have a stable banking, financial and political system.

Following is the exchange rates between the US dollar with a few representative countries' currencies:

Year	**United States**	**United Kingdom**	**Germany**	**Japan**	**China**	**India**	**Brazil**
1922	$1	0.22 Pound	430.47 Mark	2.09 Yen	1.79 Old Yuan	3.48 Rupee	7.72 Milreis

Year	United States	United Kingdom	Germany	Japan	China	India	Brazil
1940	$1	0.26 Pound	2.49 Richsmark	4.27 Yen	16.66 New Yuan	3.32 Rupee	16.51 Old Cruzeiros
1981	$1	0.49 Pound	2.26 Deutche Mark	220.63 Yen	1.70 Yuan	9.48 Rupee	93.07 New Cruzeiros
1990	$1	0.56 Pound	1.61 Deutche Mark	145.00 Yen	4.79 Yuan	17.49 Rupee	68.30 New Cruzados
1995	$1	0.63 Pound	1.43 Deutche Mark	93.96 Yen	8.37 Yuan	32.42 Rupee	0.91 Reals
2000	$1	0.65 Pound	1.11 Euro	107.80 Yen	8.27 Yuan	45.00 Rupee	1.83 Reals
2005	$1	0.54 Pound	0.84 Euro	110.11 Yen	8.19 Yuan	44.00 Rupee	2.43
2010	$1	0.64 Pound	0.75 Euro	87.78 Yen	6.76 Yuan	45.65 Rupee	1.76 Reals
2015	$1	0.65 Pound	0.91 Euro	121.04 Yen	6.28 Yuan	64.11 Rupee	3.33 Reals

Year	United States	United Kingdom	Germany	Japan	China	India	Brazil
March 2019	$1	0.76 Pound	0.88 Euro	110.01 Yen	6.71 Yuan	68.93 Rupee	3.85 Reals

Summary

The average rate of return on commodities is about 7%, which is very similar to stock market averages. Depending on the commodity, natural disasters and man-made problems could greatly affect your investment. However, if you look at the broad picture, commodity investment can certainly be a valuable component of any portfolio.

As with all investments, make sure you do your research or consult an investment professional prior to committing your money. The information in this chapter is a very broad outline of the commodities market and how certain individual commodities react in the market. The more time you spend determining what works for you, the greater your comfort level will be with this type of investment opportunity.

CHAPTER 9

The Seductive World of Real Estate Investing

"The four most dangerous words in investing are 'This time, it's different.'"

John Templeton

Real estate is another type of investment with which to diversify your portfolio. It is also the oldest. By the early days of Greece, Plato and Aristotle discussed the merits and liabilities of owning land. Since those early historical days, owning real estate has been a staple of securing wealth. While the traditional manner of owning property is still the primary way of investing in real estate, we will look at some alternatives.

Owning Your Home

Depending on a person's income level, their house is often their single biggest asset, and the place where most of their money is tied up. To many, investing in a good house is a no-brainer. It appreciates in value and whatever improvements you put into it will be reflected in the increased value of the home. As with most conventional wisdoms, that may be true overall but does not happen every single time. As with many investments, there is more to owning your home and other pieces of real estate than meets the eye. You will see that there are lessons to owning your house that also apply to most real estate transactions.

First of all, real estate is one investment where you don't have to have all the money in your pocket in order to buy what you want. As an example, say you have your eye on a house that costs $1 million. You have $200,000 you've saved over a period of time. With a good income and credit rating, you go to a bank and get a mortgage for $800,000. Instead of taking years to save up the balance that you need to pay for the house, you now own it in a matter of months. There are not too many investments that give you the flexibility to get more than you can pay for right now.

Let's say the people who purchased that home are a married couple with two teenage children. Their game plan is to own the house for ten years. By then, the kids will be out on their own, and they can sell the house, take the profit, and either downsize or buy that beach home they always had their eye on in some resort location.

It is a good plan, but there are often factors they did not take into account. First of all, as with many investments, there are no guarantees that the price of their home will appreciate. It depends on the location and the general economic environment of the sale. Back in 2008, when the price of real estate dropped dramatically, it affected many properties all over the country. Some places like Las Vegas and Florida were hit particularly hard. Individuals found themselves in the position of selling their homes and taking a big loss.

Even if your home appreciates, you have to keep in mind what you have put into your house, and not just regular maintenance and improvements. If you took out a mortgage, you are paying interest on the money you borrowed. Even with interest rates being reasonably low, that still adds up to quite a bit of money you are paying the bank. Throw in property taxes, insurance, homeowner association fees (if applicable), and utilities, and you discover that you have a good size annual expense coming out of your pocket. When you factor that in, you may find the "windfall" that you reap when you sell your home may not be as much as you thought.

This is not being negative on home ownership by any means. It is merely to show you the way many homeowners think about the financial side of home ownership. When you hear that someone received $300,000 more on the sale of their house than they paid for it, just remember that is not their net profit. While you cannot put a price tag on the emotional attachment to a home, if you run the numbers, you may find the profit may not be as great as it first appears.

For 25 years, Yale economics professor Robert Shiller has tracked U.S. home prices. He monitors current prices, yes, but he has also researched historical prices. This graph of Shiller's data* (through January 2019) shows how housing prices have changed over time. As you can see, home prices bounced around until the mid 1910s, at which point they dropped sharply. This decline was due largely to new mass-production techniques, which lowered the cost of building a home. Prices did not recover until the conclusion of World War II and the coming of the G.I. Bill. From the 1950s until the mid-1990s, home prices hovered around 110 on the Shiller scale. For the past twenty years, the U.S. housing market has been a wild ride. We experienced an enormous bubble (and its aftermath) during the late 2000s.

*US Home Prices 1890-Present: Historical housing market data used in Robert Shiller's "Irrational Exuberance" [Princeton University Press 2000, Broadway Books 2001, 2nd edition, 2005], shows home prices since 1890, and are available for download and updated monthly.

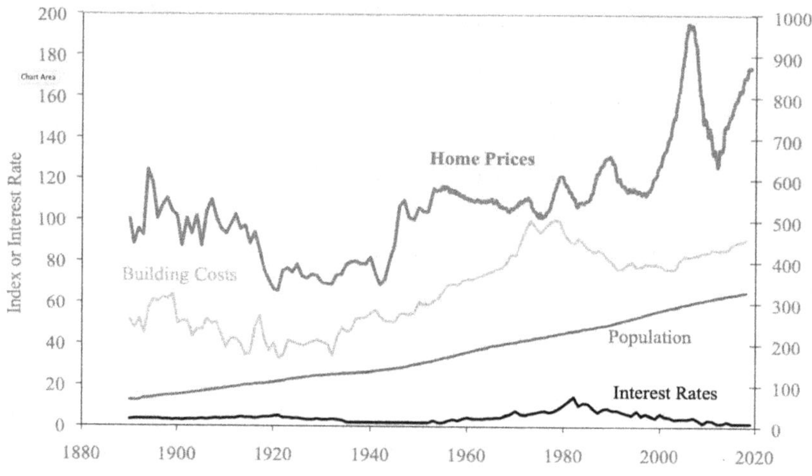

Real Estate as an Investment

Outside of owning your home, investing in real estate is a broad category of operating, investing, and financial activities centered on making money from tangible property or producing a cash flow linked to tangible property.

In its purest form, the investor is a landlord. He or she owns the land and/or building(s). That person finds someone who wants the property and charges them rent for it. There is a psychological comfort for many investors to owning property like this. They can go to the property and see what they own. They can decorate or modify it to their heart's content. They also have a certain degree of control reflective of the market and local regulations to charge what they want for the property. This becomes a very active investment, as the owners can be as involved in a property as they want.

If you are looking at real estate as an investment, you can own property in these broad categories: residential real estate, commercial real estate, industrial real estate, retail real estate, and mixed-use real estate. They each have their pros and cons, and many times it comes down to what a landlord feels comfortable owning. Since this chapter is devoted to a general overview of real estate, I suggest exploring in more detail the types of real estate ownership that might interest you. They all have their own unique benefits and drawbacks, economic characteristics and rent cycles, customary lease terms and brokerage practices.

Like with a home, a person can make real estate purchases of these types only needing a percentage of the sale price, borrowing the rest. This leverage is a major draw for investing in real estate. Let's look at a quick example to illustrate this point.

Here we have an investor using $150,000 from their savings to buy a house outright. If the house increases in value by $8,000 in one year, then the investor made a return of 5% (assuming no other costs for this example). However, if the investor obtained 70% financing, he would only need $45,000 in cash when closing on the property. The mortgage would provide the additional $105,000 needed to acquire the property.

If we assume the same $8000 in increased value, the investor's original $45,000 would yield an increase in equity of $53,000 in one year, a 15% return on investment. If he is using the house as a rental property, and you add in that income, the return is substantially higher. Even if the property value stayed stable with no appreciation, you would still see a positive return on the investment. Similarly, if property value were to go down by $8000 then you are losing 15% on your investment.

The above is a textbook example of how real estate investing can work. Please keep in mind that in the real world, you are going to have expenses on your property. An owner has to factor all those things in that we talked about with home ownership: interest, insurance, maintenance, improvements, etc. You have to take these into consideration when calculating the true cash flow from the property.

There are certain tax advantages when investing in a property. You'll have depreciation on the property. Even if the value appreciates, the government allows owners a tax deduction of their property over its lifespan. Besides the depreciation, an investor can usually claim the interest portion of his monthly mortgage payment as a tax deduction.

When embarking on real estate investments, there are some definite do's and don'ts that can keep an investor on a successful path. One of the first is not to do everything yourself. A successful real estate investor builds a team of professionals. You need to develop a good alliance with at least one real estate agent. In addition, it is a good idea to have an established relationship with an appraiser, home or building inspector, a closing attorney, and a lender or two depending on the volume of deals you conduct.

Once you have your property, you also need a team in the remodeling or maintenance side of the business: a plumber, an electrician, a roofer, a painter, heating and air conditioning professional, contractor, a flooring installer, a lawn maintenance service, a cleaning service, and an all-around handyman.

One of the biggest detriments to success in real estate investment is paying too much for the properties you acquire. Be very careful in analyzing the properties you are thinking about buying. Whether you are looking to turn it around quickly to sell or plan on receiving long-term rents, thoroughly investigate location, local real estate trends, and any other factors that could be the difference between success and failure.

Along those lines, it is important to educate yourself on real estate investments. Watching a couple shows on HGTV on how to flip houses doesn't prepare you for all the intricacies involved. Before you invest your hard-earned money, read articles, scour the Internet, check out books from the library, and look for a local chapter of the National Real Estate Investors Association. Find someone successful in real estate, who will act as a consultant or tutor to bring you up to speed on what you need to know.

You also need to do your due diligence on the actual property you want to purchase. Successful real estate investors usually have to close deals quickly. However, that doesn't mean you shouldn't look at all of the costs, potential costs, and the market conditions surrounding any one transaction. An investor can deplete his savings by purchasing a property that needs a great deal of money poured into it. This is a particularly important point for new investors, who may be tempted to overlook additional out of pocket expenses assuming they'll make up the difference if and when the property appreciates.

Another issue is if an investor does not calculate a property's cash flow properly. If the investment strategy is to buy and then rent out properties, then you need to generate a sufficient amount of money to cover maintenance and other costs, as well as have some left over for income.

Something else that might block cash flow is if an investor buys a rental property with the intention of hiring a property manager to run it. The cost of such a manager will eat away at the monthly cash income from the property. Again, do your homework before moving forward on a purchase.

The amount of deals you are working on is going to have an impact on your success or failure. It is a good idea to have a sufficient number of transactions going at any one time so that your good deals will support any marginal ones. This gives you some flexibility as you try to either improve the properties that are a problem or get rid of them.

Another way to keep a positive balance is to make sure you have multiple exit strategies for any single property you invest in. If you buy something with the intent of flipping it and that doesn't work, Plan B might be to rent it. If rents are stalling in your area, maybe offer it as a lease-purchase opportunity to a buyer. Since one of the downsides of real estate is the lack of liquidity of your investment, make sure to have several ways to generate income from it.

While we have had short discussions on knowing the hidden costs of owning property, there is one more factor many investors miscalculate: time, which is often underestimated. Things just tend to take longer than anticipated in real estate. This is everything from how long a successful rehab of a building will take to when the income from a rental property will reach a certain level. Time is money, as they say. Some experts say to double whatever your original estimate is when reaching a certain goal. If you can still live with the investment with that in mind, then it's probably a good deal for you.

In addition to outright ownership of property, there are other categories of investing in real estate. For instance, you can lease a space or property and sub-lease it to others at a higher rate than you are paying, assuming your lease allows for subletting. As an example, you lease out an office space, divide it into smaller units, and rent them out to businesses. You can achieve quite a high return on your investment if your location is conducive to something like this.

Real Estate Investment Trusts (REIT)

For an individual, who would still like to invest in real estate while avoiding the responsibilities of actually being a landlord, he or she can buy into a real estate investment trust. REITs have a unique tax structure and became an alternative real estate investment in the 1960's. They came about to encourage smaller investors to invest in real estate projects they otherwise wouldn't be able to afford, such as building shopping centers or hotels.

A REIT is similar to a mutual fund in the way it works. You are investing in a portfolio of properties rather than a single building. You buy shares of a REIT, and your gain or loss depends on the performance of those properties as a whole. If one or two of the properties underperform, the hope is the remainder of the portfolio more than makes up for them. It spreads out the risk to the investor's dollar. In addition to the diversity, another important advantage of REITs is their liquidity. Unlike actual real estate, REIT shares allow you to quickly and easily sell your shares.

Summary

This is only a general outline on real estate investing. It takes years of practice, experience, patience and exposure to truly appreciate, understand, and master. Remember that real estate is only one component of your diversified portfolio. How much money you put into it is going to depend on how much you are investing overall. You may find it is sufficient to invest in one or two additional properties besides your home. You might also decide that being a landlord doesn't suit you at all, and that owning shares in one or more REITs works best for you.

As with any investment, buying and selling properties come with risk. The value of your investment will go up and down. Even though the track record of real estate is one of steady appreciation, the market over the past 10 years illustrates there are no guarantees. Many times combining the real estate investment with cash value life insurance (we'll discuss shortly) will provide the multiple tax advantages and ability to put your money to multiple uses.

CHAPTER 10

The Dull Investment of Life Insurance

"Beware the investment activity that produces applause; the great moves are usually greeted by yawns."

Warren Buffett

As with many things we've discussed so far, life insurance has its origins in ancient Rome. Back then, they had "burial clubs" that provided funds for a member's funeral, as well as some assistance to the deceased's survivors. A London company, the Amicable Society for a Perpetual Assurance Office, began in 1706 with 2,000 members and was the forerunner to today's life insurance companies. Life insurance became available in the United States while it was still a British colony. The Presbyterian Synods in Philadelphia and New York City created the Corporation for Relief of Poor and Distressed Widows and Children of Presbyterian Ministers in 1759. Two dozen life insurance companies sprang up between 1787 and 1837. Other companies formed after that leading to the many companies we have in existence today offering various types of life insurance products.

When you are establishing a plan to invest and protect your income, life insurance should be an important consideration. Life insurance is a replacement of income that can continue to support the dependents of an insured individual after that person has passed away. In addition to this primary purpose, life insurance is a powerful investment and tax-planning vehicle. We'll explore the investment side of a life insurance policy.

Types of Life Insurance

There are two basic types of life insurance policies for you to consider. One is temporary, such as a term life policy. Then there is permanent life insurance represented by whole life, universal, and variable life policies.

Term insurance is similar to renting an apartment for a certain period of time. Once that "term" expires, you either find a new place to live or pay more in rent. A term policy works the same way – when you reach the end of the term, your insurance protection ends, and there is no cash value.

As the name implies, if you die because of any reason within the defined term – maybe in 10 years, 20 years or maximum 30 years – the insurance company will pay the death benefit to your beneficiary. If you do not die during the defined term period, then your life insurance premium is gone forever – very much like your car insurance premium. Term insurance suits someone who needs substantial life insurance, but does not have a lot of money to spend. Another way to look at term insurance is that it is a temporary solution similar to renting an apartment until you are ready to move into a house.

A cash value life insurance policy by comparison is similar to owning your own home. In this policy, premiums are larger than term policy premiums, just as mortgage payments are higher than rent, but you end up owning a life insurance policy with a cash value to utilize for any living needs. A permanent life policy covers you for the rest of your life. It builds cash value similar to increased equity in your home. It also enjoys income and estate tax advantages that give greater flexibility with your total investment plan. It can be used as a college savings plan, a retirement plan, or any other purpose you choose.

There is an ongoing debate about whether term or cash value life insurance is the better option. There is no easy answer to that, as no one size fits all. The best type of life insurance policy for you depends on your unique circumstances. You have to take into consideration many factors when making this decision. Age, health, financial responsibility, other financial assets and your personal opinion influence the decision.

Always remember that the purpose of life insurance is to provide cash for your family, your business or yourself. It can help create wealth when you have not had time to do so, and it can help protect your estate from taxes when you have accumulated a lot of money. Even though cash value life insurance has many advantages, it may not be appropriate for everyone's personal financial situation. Let's look a little more in-depth at two kinds of investment-grade cash value life insurance – whole life insurance and indexed universal life.

Whole Life Insurance

Whole life insurance provides three guarantees: premium, death benefit and cash value inside the policy. A whole life policy provides a decent internal rate of return (net to all the costs and expenses) of approximately 4% to 5% NET over the long-term period, usually 20 years or more. Whole life insurance also gives you the peace of mind that life insurance will always be there as long as the guaranteed premiums are paid.

As you pay premiums into your policy, it accumulates a cash value or equity in your policy (or in an account). Fueling this growth inside your policy are the dividends paid by the life insurance companies to your policy. Your premium will remain the same for life, and you will have a choice of paying premiums for that duration, whether it be for 7 years, 10 years, 15 years, or until you retire.

The cash value that builds up in a whole life policy (the equity) allows you some flexibility with how to use your policy. As long as there is at least some cash value in your whole life insurance policy, you can withdraw it anytime, very much like a savings account in a bank. Part of each premium payment accumulates in this account and continues to grow tax-deferred as long as the policy exists. You can withdraw your entire cash value tax-free via a loan strategy.

The cash value that builds up inside your policy is creditor-proof in most states. This makes whole life insurance a sort of double-indemnity policy by not only protecting your family should you die suddenly, but also, by protecting your family if someone sues you, or you have to declare bankruptcy.

There is no stock market link or a volatility associated with this kind of a policy, but the insurance company provides a fixed return for your premium dollars. There are only a few whole life insurance companies left. They have paid dividends for their whole life policies since their existence and most of them are a century and half old. Their typical dividend rate is around 6 to 7% and the net return comes to around 4.5 to 5% after all expenses are accounted for. Following is the last three decades of dividend history from some of whole life insurance companies:

Year	MassMutual	Penn Mutual	New York Life	Guardian Life	Ohio National	Northwestern Mutual
2018	6.4	6.34	6.2	5.85	5.4	4.9
2017	6.7	6.34	6.2	5.85	5.75	5
2016	7.1	6.34	6.2	6.05	6	5.45
2015	7.1	6.34	6.2	6.05	6	5.6
2014	7.1	6.34	6	6.25	6	5.6
2013	7	6.34	5.9	6.65	6	5.6
2012	7	6.34	5.8	6.95	6.15	5.85
2011	6.85	6.34	6.11	6.85	6.15	6
2010	7	6.34	6.11	7	6.4	6.15
2009	7.6	6.34	6.14	7.3	6.4	6.5
2008	7.9	6.34	6.79	7.25	6.65	7.5
2007	7.5	6.3	6.79	6.75	6.65	7.5
2006	7.4	6.3	6.79	6.5	6.65	7.5
2005	7	5.74	6.79	6.75	6.9	7.5
2004	7.5	5.74	6.79	6.6	7.4	7.7
2003	7.9	6.48	6.79	7	7.7	8.2
2002	8.05	7.4	7.32	8	7.7	8.6
2001	8.2	7.4	7.9	8.5	8.3	8.8
2000	8.2	7.4	7.9	8.5	8.3	8.8
1999	8.4	7.4	7.9	8.75	N/A	8.8
1998	8.4	8	7.9	8.75	N/A	8.8
1997	8.4	8	7.9	8.5	N/A	8.5
1996	8.4	8.5	7.9	8	N/A	8.5
1995	9	8.5	8.25	8.5	N/A	8.5
1994	9.3	9.2	8.5	9	N/A	8.5
1993	9.45	9.7	8.05	9.75	N/A	9.25
1992	9.95	9.93	8.9	10.25	N/A	9.25
1991	10.5	9.93	9.75	10.5	N/A	10
1990	10.5	9.93	10.25	11	N/A	10
1989	11.15	9.93	10.25	11.5	N/A	10

One negative of whole life insurance is there is no upside potential such as in the stock market, as its return is guaranteed like a CD.

Indexed Universal Life Insurance

Indexed Universal Life is the latest innovation in the cash value life insurance world. It's a hybrid product where you are able to link your return with various stock market indices such the S & P 500, Nasdaq 100, DJIA, EURO STIXX 50, Bloomberg Barclay U.S. Aggregate Bond etc., but with the security of general accounts of whole life insurance.

As per the graphic below, almost 95% of premiums invested in insurance companies' general accounts yields around 5% annually. That means 95% becomes your original premium amount at the end of the year. Of the remaining 5%, first, insurance mortality and other administrative expenses are taken out, and the remaining money is left for what are called option hedge strategies. If corresponding stock or bond indices close in the negative, then the option expires worthless. If it closes positively, then the option is "in the money," and that return is shared with the policyholder as a dividend. This eliminates any losses, while allowing the owner to participate in the upside of the stock market, with a cap on the return, such as 12%.

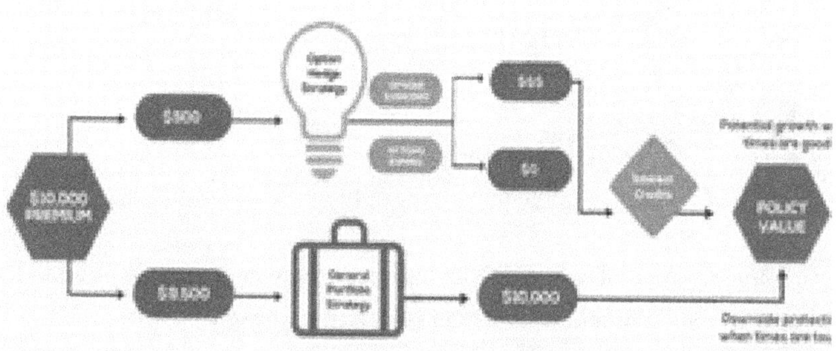

By limiting loss to zero indexed Univeral Life insurance enhances return even with the growth participation cap at 12%. Please see below comparison of actual S&P 500 index return with zero floor and 12% cap since the inception in 1957. The actual return is 6.86%, while cap and floor strategy produce 7.02% return.

Please see on the next page a comparison of actual S&P 500 index returns with zero floor and 12% cap from 1960 to 1980, when the return was not so attractive. The actual return is 3.97%, while the cap and floor strategy produces 6.37% return.

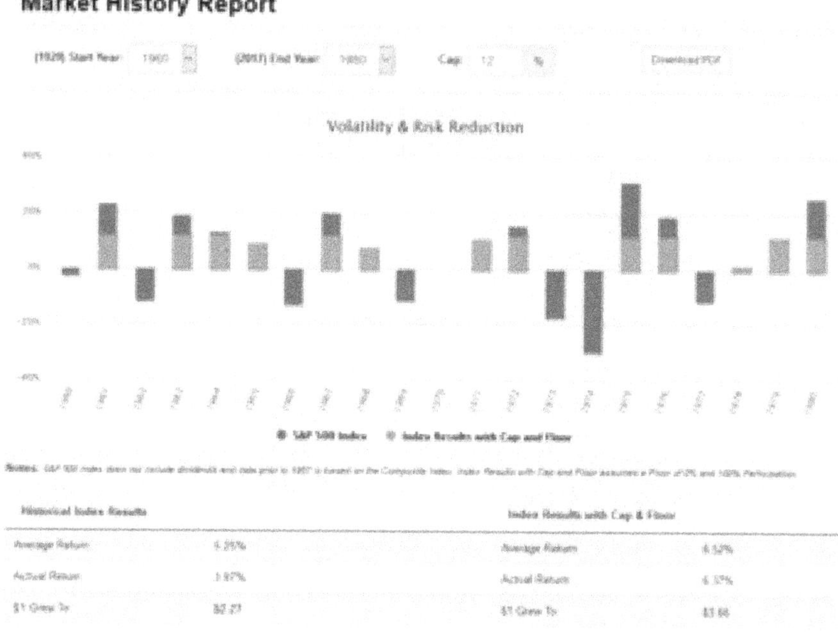

Finally, please see the comparison of the actual S&P 500 index return with zero floor and 12% cap in down market from 2000 to 2010. The actual return is 1.41%, while cap and floor strategy produces 5.64% return.

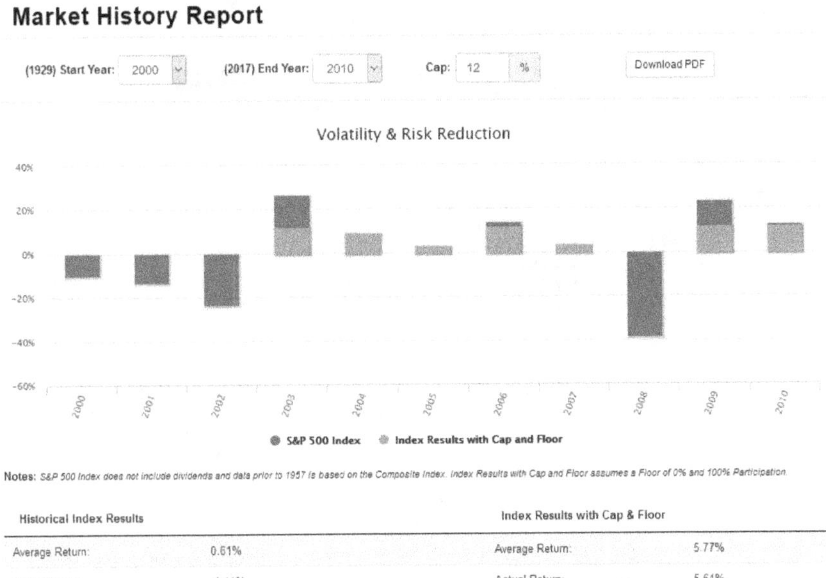

Historical Index Results		Index Results with Cap & Floor	
Average Return:	0.61%	Average Return:	5.77%
Actual Return:	-1.41%	Actual Return:	5.64%
$1 Grew To:	$0.86	$1 Grew To:	$1.83

There is no mutual fund management fees as they are not actually investing in the funds, but only buying the option of various stock and bond indexes. Finally, see on the following page an illustration of the power of combining two economic powers of accumulation and distribution rates with section 7702 tax advantages. The following comparison of Premium life is a concept of indexed universal life insurance and taxable account with investment in S&P 500 index with the same investment return and expenses.

PremiumLife

End Year	Age	POLICY PREMIUM	TAX FREE INCOME	YIELD	YEAR END ACCUM VALUE	YEAR END SURR VALUE	DEATH BENEFIT
1	50	60,000	0	6.50%	49,318	0	2,296,318
2	51	60,000	0	6.50%	100,941	29,236	2,367,941
3	52	60,000	0	6.50%	154,862	84,676	2,361,862
4	53	60,000	0	6.50%	212,956	142,977	2,419,956
5	54	60,000	0	6.50%	273,891	205,369	2,480,891
6	55	60,000	0	6.50%	338,426	272,861	2,545,426
7	56	60,000	0	6.50%	408,567	343,593	2,615,567
8	57	60,000	0	6.50%	483,876	429,758	2,690,876
9	58	60,000	0	6.50%	564,613	521,312	2,771,613
10	59	60,000	0	6.50%	653,786	621,299	2,860,786
11	60	60,000	0	6.50%	749,552	737,861	2,956,552
12	61	60,000	0	6.50%	852,476	841,862	3,059,476
13	62	60,000	0	6.50%	969,931	969,931	3,176,931
14	63	60,000	0	6.50%	1,096,166	1,096,166	3,303,166
15	64	60,000	0	6.50%	1,231,836	1,231,836	3,438,836
16	65	0	0	6.50%	1,320,246	1,320,246	3,267,680
17	66	0	125,000	6.50%	1,414,059	1,283,299	2,079,750
18	67	0	125,000	6.50%	1,514,880	1,249,816	1,907,836
19	68	0	125,000	6.50%	1,622,888	1,208,240	1,793,234
20	69	0	125,000	6.50%	1,736,392	1,170,688	1,641,296
21	70	0	125,000	6.50%	1,858,674	1,133,639	1,481,761
22	71	0	125,000	6.50%	1,989,623	1,096,873	1,395,316
23	72	0	125,000	6.50%	2,129,761	1,061,112	1,337,980
24	73	0	125,000	6.50%	2,279,182	1,029,862	1,276,572
25	74	0	125,000	6.50%	2,438,646	991,419	1,219,888
26	75	0	125,000	6.50%	2,608,984	958,118	1,140,743
27	76	0	125,000	6.50%	2,791,137	926,496	1,068,865
28	77	0	125,000	6.50%	2,989,241	896,119	1,046,381
29	78	0	125,000	6.50%	3,192,038	867,299	1,026,811
30	79	0	125,000	6.50%	3,412,329	840,005	1,010,621
TOTALS		900,000	1,750,000				

TAXABLE INVESTMENT

End Year	Age	DEPOSIT	AFTER TAX CASH FLOW 30% TAX RATE	YIELD	PRE TAX INCOME	YEAR END ACCOUNT VALUE
1	50	60,000	0	6.50%	3,900	62,730
2	51	60,000	0	6.50%	7,977	128,294
3	52	60,000	0	6.50%	12,246	196,883
4	53	60,000	0	6.50%	16,651	268,371
5	54	60,000	0	6.50%	21,367	343,521
6	55	60,000	0	6.50%	26,329	421,881
7	56	60,000	0	6.50%	31,322	503,866
8	57	60,000	0	6.50%	36,847	589,464
9	58	60,000	0	6.50%	42,215	679,618
10	59	60,000	0	6.50%	48,036	772,636
11	60	60,000	0	6.50%	54,121	870,520
12	61	60,000	0	6.50%	60,484	972,048
13	62	60,000	0	6.50%	67,136	1,079,854
14	63	60,000	0	6.50%	74,098	1,191,717
15	64	60,000	0	6.50%	81,362	1,308,639
16	65	0	0	6.50%	85,044	1,368,214
17	66	0	125,000	6.50%	88,939	1,299,781
18	67	0	125,000	6.50%	76,361	1,238,232
19	68	0	125,000	6.50%	71,719	1,153,438
20	69	0	125,000	6.50%	66,848	1,075,224
21	70	0	125,000	6.50%	61,746	993,468
22	71	0	125,000	6.50%	56,459	907,974
23	72	0	125,000	6.50%	50,861	818,681
24	73	0	125,000	6.50%	45,884	725,152
25	74	0	125,000	6.50%	39,810	627,466
26	75	0	125,000	6.50%	32,660	525,327
27	76	0	125,000	6.50%	26,621	410,542
28	77	0	125,000	6.50%	19,888	300,899
29	78	0	125,000	6.50%	11,623	190,175
30	79	0	125,000	6.50%	4,336	68,148
TOTALS		900,000	1,750,000			

End Year	Age	POLICY PREMIUM	TAX FREE INCOME	YIELD	YEAR END ACCUM VALUE	YEAR END SURR VALUE	DEATH BENEFIT
31	80	0	125,000	6.50%	3,546,946	816,760	997,907
32	81	0	125,000	6.50%	3,896,787	791,722	986,508
33	82	0	125,000	6.50%	4,162,616	771,060	979,199
34	83	0	125,000	6.50%	4,445,418	753,643	975,314
35	84	0	125,000	6.50%	4,746,118	737,874	975,180
36	85	0	125,000	6.50%	5,065,575	725,668	976,547
37	86	0	125,000	6.50%	5,404,564	716,383	986,420
38	87	0	125,000	6.50%	5,763,434	709,625	997,796
39	88	0	125,000	6.50%	6,143,530	706,781	1,012,967
40	89	0	125,000	6.50%	6,546,023	704,136	1,031,387
41	90	0	125,000	6.50%	6,968,168	703,987	1,052,396
42	91	0	125,000	6.50%	7,413,026	704,368	1,075,839
43	92	0	125,000	6.50%	7,880,636	713,313	1,028,868
44	93	0	125,000	6.50%	8,399,646	734,307	986,296
45	94	0	125,000	6.50%	8,962,237	772,381	951,426
46	95	0	125,000	6.50%	9,564,213	834,154	929,666
47	96	0	125,000	6.50%	10,214,894	927,541	927,541
48	97	0	125,000	6.50%	10,921,537	1,038,566	1,038,566
49	98	0	125,000	6.50%	11,677,405	1,169,836	1,169,836
50	99	0	125,000	6.50%	12,485,998	1,320,960	1,320,960
51	100	0	125,000	6.50%	13,351,879	1,496,629	1,496,629
			4,375,000				

End Year	Age	DEPOSIT	AFTER TAX CASH FLOW 30% TAX RATE	YIELD	PRE TAX INCOME	YEAR END ACCOUNT VALUE
31	80	0	68,140	6.50%	0	0
32	81	0	0	6.50%	0	0
33	82	0	0	6.50%	0	0
34	83	0	0	6.50%	0	0
35	84	0	0	6.50%	0	0
36	85	0	0	6.50%	0	0
37	86	0	0	6.50%	0	0
38	87	0	0	6.50%	0	0
39	88	0	0	6.50%	0	0
40	89	0	0	6.50%	0	0
41	90	0	0	6.50%	0	0
42	91	0	0	6.50%	0	0
43	92	0	0	6.50%	0	0
44	93	0	0	6.50%	0	0
45	94	0	0	6.50%	0	0
46	95	0	0	6.50%	0	0
47	96	0	0	6.50%	0	0
48	97	0	0	6.50%	0	0
49	98	0	0	6.50%	0	0
50	99	0	0	6.50%	0	0
51	100	0	0	6.50%	0	0
			1,818,140			

Summary

The cash value life insurance is probably the most misunderstood investment vehicle. We are used to allocating any type of insurance into an expense category, and that is true about term life insurance, but one needs to look at any financial instrument based on its utility rather than its name or type of service. Most people think that the term insurance is the cheapest, and it is true in the short run but it gets more and more expensive as you own it. In the Penn State University's 1993 study, close to only one percent collect death benefits. Term insurance failed to take advantage of one of the most important benefits of life insurance, the tax-deferred growth and tax free withdrawal under IRS Section 7702. Term insurance has its necessity when one needs the coverage, but it does not have any cash flow to pay a premium like the cash value life insurance provides. It does not mean all types of cash value life insurance are worth considering. In fact, variable universal life insurance is probably the kind of cash value life insurance that should be avoided based on the investment expenses of underlying separate accounts. Similar to managed mutual funds, the cash value life insurance shares the same tax advantages.

As I wrote about in the chapter five, there are three factors that affect investment returns during the accumulation stage of your money – asset allocation, taxation and expenses. The cash value life insurance creates the perfect storm by incorporating these benefits. Ultimately, isn't the purpose of any long term savings and investment is to create retirement income, liquidity and an inheritance for the family?

The cash value life insurance combines the second economic power of actuarial science to almost double retirement income distribution and create substantial tax-efficient legacy for the family. You will learn more about this in chapters twelve and fourteen. That being said, cash value life insurance is a long term investment vehicle, and proper care must be taken before you implement this strategy.

For most individuals with financial means, large corporations and banks have understood the value of cash value life insurance. Recent industry surveys show that 75% of the Fortune 1000 companies have Corporate Owned Life Insurance (COLI) plans in place, and almost 3800 banks in the United States own $189 billion in bank owned life insurance (BOLI) policies using cash value life insurance primarily for their better rate of return and tax advantages, even though, corporations and banks have limited tax benefits compare to individual ownership.

CHAPTER 11

Estate Planning for All

"Death is not the end. There remains the litigation over the estate."

Ambrose Bierce

Let's go back to that old saying that the only thing certain in life are death and taxes. The scary thing is that if you do not arrange your affairs in the correct way, those you leave behind may have to pay taxes after your death. While it is not something we will worry about when we move on from this life, most of us do not want our loved ones left with a financial burden to deal with.

Your Will

This is a topic many people want to avoid. I understand those feelings.

But there are various reasons for having a last will and testament. Whatever your motivation, a will is the device that makes sure your final wishes and the distribution of your assets occur according to your desires. If you die without a will, what happens to your estate is subject to the laws of whatever state in which you reside. When I first heard that, I went out and had my first will prepared. I don't know about the state you live in, but I don't have a lot of confidence leaving those matters up to my state! After all, a state's rules might designate that everything goes to your closest blood relative. It could be a person you choose not to have a relationship with for the past twenty-five years. Also, estate taxes tend to be a larger proportion of your remaining assets if you do not set up a will, and you are leaving a substantial inheritance.

Before we get into the financial aspects of a will, I want to remind you that a will does more than ensure that the people you want to receive your assets actually receive them. If you have minor children, a will states your wishes of who should raise them. (It is always a good idea to clear this with the potential guardians first to make sure they are in a position to care for your minor children.) Many people now have a "living will" as a separate document. This is where you give instructions to medical personnel or designated individuals on what to do if you are on life support. It prevents people from pulling the plug, or leaving it in too long if you are in a condition where you cannot communicate.

When you are ready to construct your will, look for an attorney experienced in this field. A will's complexity is guided by your final wishes and the size of your estate. Some wills are fairly simple and inexpensive to write. There are web-based companies that specialize in legal documents that can help you complete a will for a modest fee. In other cases, the document might be very long and incorporate different financial vehicles you establish to make the transfer of your wealth easy for all concerned, and at a minimal tax rate. If you can take care of most contingencies while you are alive, the better it will be for your survivors.

Choosing an executor for your will is a good start when you begin the process. This person is the manager of your will. He or she knows where to find the will, implements your final wishes, and makes sure distribution of your estate occurs according to your instructions. Just as in the case of choosing guardians for your children, discuss the topic with the person you want for your executor to make sure they are prepared to handle the responsibility before putting them in this role.

I know that this is not a subject many of us want to spend a great deal of time talking about. However, a will provides you with a sense of peace knowing that you are taking care of some tough decisions. You are also taking care of your family. You can make an impact at your church or favorite charities. Many people wish to leave some type of legacy behind; this will be your last chance to do so.

Your will can also leave instructions on how to pay any estate taxes and other debts you might leave behind. If constructed properly, your will can reduce taxes and costs. Quite often, other legal devices are established in conjunction with your will or developed ahead of time. This is where the "planning" of estate planning comes in. Often, it might mean the cooperation of several different types of experts working together to produce a blueprint of what you want to happen. Estate planners, attorneys, insurance and financial specialists, accountants, etc. could all have a part to play in setting up the estate you want to leave behind.

Estate and Gift Taxes

Planning is very important because the taxes that the government levies on your estate can be very high. You might think that you are leaving your heirs in good shape after you go, but if not planned out properly, you could leave them with a prohibitive financial burden. You would think that a logical consideration would be to give assets away while one is still alive, but then you have to deal with the restrictions of the gift tax. The government is exceedingly good at figuring out how to tax our assets to the very end!

When you think of your estate, you have to include everything. This means your home and other properties, all bank accounts, business interests, pensions, jewelry, investments in any form, etc. The list is very extensive and many people are surprised at how much they are worth when they take the time to do the math of what they own.

As for estate taxes, they can be applied to various assets. Federal estate taxes are computed on the gross amount of the estate. Real property, investments, savings, and business interests go into the total. If you own property jointly with a spouse or significant other, one-half interest in pensions, savings, and real property will be part of the estate total.

If you decide to gift anything you own to family, friends, or an organization, be sure to double check what you want to give and how you plan on doing it. Taxes could fall on both the giver and the receiver if certain guidelines are not met. This book is not meant to be an exhaustive list on all the potential taxes you could encounter, but I certainly want to make sure you are aware of what you could face if you have a sizable estate. Find a professional you can trust to help you with these decisions.

Just to give you an idea of how taxes can affect you, the estate and gift tax exemption for 2019 increased to $11,400,000 per individual and the tax rate fixed at 40%. This means that if you have an estate of $15 million without your spouse alive, your heirs are responsible for paying a substantial tax on the remaining amount after the exemption amount. Keep in mind that there is a good chance you already paid all other taxes on some or all of this amount while you were alive!

Estate Planning Options

As a person looks at their personal situation, some methods of planning for the distribution of the estate will make more sense than others. Here are a number of options to keep in mind when you look at your assets and how you want to take care of their distribution. You might want to include some of these in your planning. Some choices offer tax savings advantages while you are alive. Each of these topics could headline their own book, so do further research and ask questions of a professional for more details.

1. Private Foundation – generally established by individuals and families with a high net worth to take advantage of charitable giving and subsequent tax savings while retaining partial control over the assets.

2. Fractional Interest Gift – a person can utilize gift and estate tax rules to give an interest in real property to a designee.

3. Charitable Remainder Interest Trust – allows an individual to move property to a trust that will go to a charity. It allows a person to take a charitable deduction on income taxes, bypass capital gains on transferred property, and keep a stream of revenue from the donated property.

4. Children's or Grandchildren's Irrevocable Education Trust – established by parents or grandparents for the specific purpose of children's education.

5. Family Limited Partnership – protects partnership property from the creditors of a partner, allows gifts to parents and children, and lessens the amount of the transfer tax value of property.

6. Irrevocable Life Insurance Trust – prevents estate taxes on insurance proceeds received at the death of an insured.

7. Health Care Power of Attorney – this allows you to name the person who will make decisions related to your healthcare if you are unable to do so.

8. Durable Power of Attorney – you name the person or firm to man-

age your money and property.

9. Annual Gift Tax Exclusion – enables you to give gifts of money or property while avoiding estate and gift taxes.

10. Revocable Living Trust – circumvents probate and allows a say in property management during life and after passing away.

More about Trusts

If you have a family and your net worth is substantial, setting up a trust is one of the most important things you can do for your loved ones. A trust is something that can help you accomplish your financial goals such as managing assets, controlling the distribution of your estate, minimizing estate tax, or protecting your property. As you can see in the list above, trusts can come in many forms and are designed for meeting specific goals.

A trust is a legal entity that holds assets for the benefit of another. You can put almost anything in a trust, such as stocks, bonds, life insurance policies, real estate, valuable antiques, or even cash. As the grantor or creator of the trust, you can put whatever you want in it, and you can name whomever you please to have access to those assets in the case of your death. The different types of trusts help individuals meet different goals, such as generating income by putting bonds in a trust, or providing cash for beneficiaries to pay estate taxes by adding a life insurance policy in it. An appointed trustee can manage the assets and distribute them to the beneficiaries per your instructions.

Besides utilizing a trust to leave your assets in the proper hands after you pass away, it can also be quite beneficial to reduce estate taxes, protect assets from potential creditors, circumvent the time and expense of probating your will, and preserve assets for minor children until they are grown. In addition, a trust can create investment pools that professional money managers can manage, support you if you are incapacitated, shift part of your income tax burden to beneficiaries in lower tax brackets, provide benefits for charity, and protect your assets.

There are three main types of trusts: the living trust or the revocable trust, the irrevocable trust, and the testamentary trust. They each have specific characteristics and we will take a quick look at their highlights.

The living trust or revocable trust is a legal entity that you create while you are alive to own property such as your house, a boat, a business, or your bank accounts. Property that passes through a living trust is not subject to probate; hence, the properties are transferred to your beneficiary immediately. The living trust is attractive because it is revocable. You maintain control over it, and you can change the trust or even dissolve it for as long as you live. Living trusts are also private. Unlike a will, a living trust is not part of the public record. No one can review details of the trust documents unless you allow it.

As the name implies, the person who establishes an irrevocable trust, unless the beneficiary of the trust grants permission, cannot change the trust. Minimizing estate taxes are the main reasons for starting such a trust. Anything placed in the irrevocable trust is removed from the grantor's estate. By the same token, the grantor also does not receive any of the income generated from the trust while he or she is living. An irrevocable trust can hold a business, investments, life insurance, and other assets.

The testamentary trusts are activated by the originator's death under his or her will and trust provisions. A testamentary trust is a legal arrangement created to oversee any assets designated for the trust. This could be any investments, life insurance proceeds, or other sources of cash. The trust documents should name a trustee to direct its administration until a trust expires. At times, the deceased is allowed to leave a letter of instruction for the trustee. Unlike the other trusts, the motivation for setting up a testamentary trust is not primarily for estate tax purposes, but for the needs of the beneficiaries of the trust. Usually, such trusts are set up to provide an ongoing source of income for minor children or for their future education.

These trusts all have variations to suit different needs. Since trusts are legal entities, a knowledgeable attorney in estate planning is necessary in setting one up. You can customize a trust to meet your desires, so be sure to have it set up properly right from the beginning.

Life Insurance

In the last chapter, I talked about life insurance primarily as an investment vehicle while you are alive. I need to point out that in certain cases, the estate tax can affect the proceeds from life insurance. If your estate is more than the current $11.4 million exemption amount, and you are the owner (rather than a trust owning it) of any insurance policies at the time of your death, the death proceeds of those policies can be part of the taxable amount of your estate.

Life insurance plays a vital role in estate creation if you don't have much in the estate. It also helps minimize the estate tax if you have a substantial estate. A permanent life insurance policy is also a great way to pay for any potential estate tax liability with the lowest cost compared to any other means. Potential estate tax needs to be paid within nine months of the death of the estate holder. Life insurance policy death benefits create instant liquidity to pay for estate taxes, alleviating your heirs from having to sell any other assets at a discount trying to quickly raise the necessary funds to pay the estate taxes.

Summary

Throughout this book, I advocate finding professionals who are successful in their field to help with your investment and tax planning. Arguably, estate planning is the most important area where this comes into play. This chapter lightly scratches the surface on the subject.

What I do want to impart is that estate planning is a vital and complex component of your total financial planning. In some ways, it is an area where the more assets you accumulate, the more attention you have to pay to how you structure your will and financial plans. Because of the different aspects of estate taxes, individual state probate laws, and assorted other details, be sure to surround yourself with people who understand how it all works together. Keep in mind that a lawyer does not necessarily know everything about how life insurance works and vice versa. That's why you need to bring in separate specialists to work on your entire estate planning picture.

One more word here on estate planning. We as human beings are always reluctant to talk about death. However, we haven't figured out a way to defeat Father Time yet, so don't be afraid to discuss these matters with the people that count in your life. Your family is number one, but the discussion might also include business partners, charities you support, etc. It is important that, whatever you decide to do in your will, those you leave behind understand any trusts or other financial methods you utilize. When we die, we have nothing to worry about here anymore…they do. You will have peace that everything you worked for is in good hands, when those closest to you know how you are taking care of them and what they will have to do when the time comes..

CHAPTER 12

IRS Section 7702 Individual Private Pension Plan

"The business schools reward difficult, complex behavior more than simple behavior, but simple behavior is more effective."

Warren Buffett

Whenever you look at ways to save money for your retirement, it's important to be mindful of certain tax advantages, in addition to the rate of return you receive on your money. The three big benefits you would like to optimize are not paying taxes on the money you are saving, not having to pay taxes on any interest you earn on that money while it is in some type of plan, and not paying taxes when you take out that money to spend it. One of these would be nice, but if you can get two out of three, you are doing very well. If you can find any financial vehicle that does three out of three, let me know.

When you invest your money that gives you at least two of these advantages, you often sacrifice ease of liquidity with whatever vehicle you choose. You can understand why they work that way. Retirement plans encourage savings for when your working days are over. If the cash were easy to get hold of, it would be too tempting to withdraw your money before retirement, and there might be nothing left for when you are no longer bringing home an income.

Background

To help understand the options presented in this chapter, it is first necessary to look at one of the newer regulations set out by the IRS. While reading IRS regulations is not anyone's idea of fun, they allow you to see the logic of certain investments for your situation.

IRS Sec 7702 deals with the accumulation of life insurance policy cash value or account value. Prior to the writing of Section 7702, federal tax law took a fairly hands-off approach when it came to the taxation of life insurance policies. One could place an unlimited amount of money into a life insurance contract that offered a tax-free death benefit, tax-deferred growth of policy account value (interest and gains that build up within the policy were not included as part of the policyholder's current income), and tax-free distribution of the cash value via a loan. This type of policy presented a problem to the IRS since people were using such life insurance vehicles to invest their money and take advantage of the generous tax breaks given to insurance policies.

Section 7702 was created to limit the tax benefits provided by life insurance policies. It did this by defining what would be considered a life insurance policy. Investment vehicles that didn't fall under the insurance definition were not eligible for the favorable tax treatments. In short, it kept most of the tax benefits, but limited how much money you can stock into the life insurance policy. This does not, however, eliminate the use of whole life and universal life insurance as an alternative means to accumulate wealth and plan for retirement while reaping the favorable tax benefits life insurance enjoys.

Tax Treatment of Any Investments

Three tax benefits exist: 1) tax-deductible contributions, 2) tax-deferred growth, and 3) tax-free withdrawal of growth.

Most investments such as CDs, brokerage accounts, and savings accounts only enjoy one of these three tax benefits, and that is tax-free withdrawal of growth.

Traditional qualified plans such as IRA, 401K, 403b, SEP, Simple Plan, Profit Sharing and Defined Benefit Plans enjoy tax-deductible contributions and tax-deferred growth, but the 100% withdrawal will be taxed at the marginal income tax rate after the age of 59.5 of the investor. If taken before the age of 59.5, there will be an additional 10% excise penalty on the entire withdrawal.

The Roth IRA, the Roth 401K and a cash value life insurance policy (as governed by the IRS Sec 7702), enjoy the tax-deferred growth of the account value, and you can withdrawal the entire account tax-free. In the case of Roth plans, the withdrawal should be after the investor turns fifty-nine and a half or five years after starting the plan, whichever is later. For the cash value of a life insurance policy, no such restrictions exist and can be taken out any time.

Two specific investment vehicles – real estate and municipal bonds – are taxed a little bit differently. Real estate primarily allows tax-deferred growth up to a certain dollar limit tax-free if it is the primary residence. Municipal bonds partially act like Roth plans and the cash value of life insurance policy. Earnings on municipal bonds are income tax free (only pay federal income tax unless the investor lives in the same state and/or city of the municipal bond), but the growth in the principal (if any) will be subject to capital gains if it is held more than a year, and ordinary income tax if held less than a year.

Traditional IRA/401K Vs. Roth IRA/401k

With a traditional IRA, 401K, and other defined contributions (Profit Sharing Plan and SEP) and defined benefits plans, you get a tax deduction up front. The taxes you pay on that income are delayed until you withdraw your money during retirement. Roth IRA, 401k, and the cash value of a life insurance policy, on the other hand, are funded with post-tax money, but the growth and withdrawal are tax-free.

So, the question is, which one is better? The answer is not simple, and it depends on many factors such as your current income tax bracket, net worth, other investment holdings, time to retire, and your ability to bite the bullet now or later.

"With a traditional IRA, you're at the mercy or uncertainty of what future higher tax rates might do to your retirement savings," according to IRA expert Ed Slott, founder of Ed Slott & Co. "With a Roth, you don't have to worry about future rates, because your tax rate in retirement will be zero."

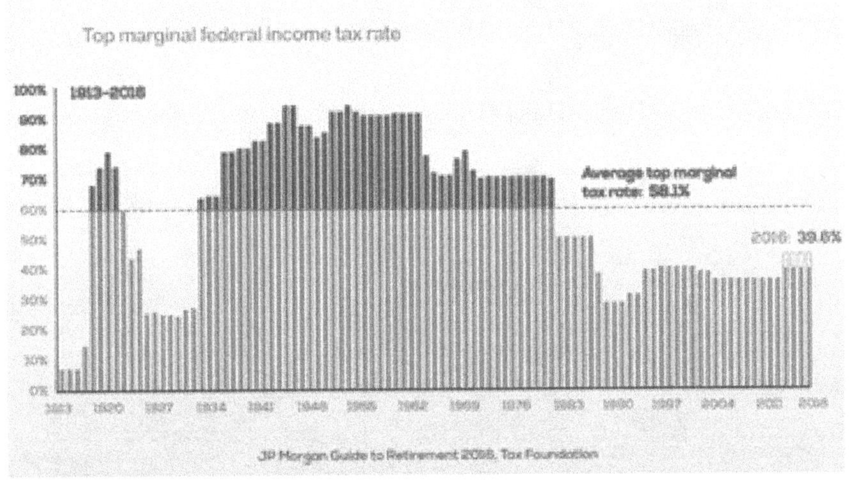

Most expert financial planners/advisors agree that over the long term, a Roth IRA is better than a traditional IRA because it is better to be taxed on the "seed" money than the "harvest" money. Also, the current national debt of $22 trillion without unfunded liabilities such as Social Security, Medicare, and the budget deficit could be a danger to future tax rates.

Historically, we are now living in the lowest tax-rate environment. The average top marginal tax-rate since 1913 has been 58%. While the current national debt is $22 trillion, when you factor in the unfunded liabilities (following GAAP accounting standards, as most public companies do), then this number is above $100 trillion – almost $1 million of debt per tax-payer. Someday we will have to deal with this debt, and there are only two logical ways to do so: 1) Reduce spending and/or 2) Increase revenue.

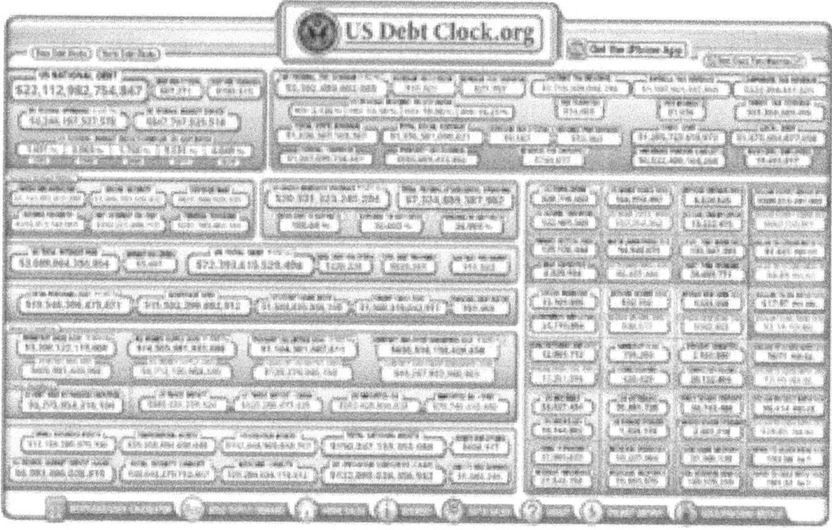

Perhaps there is a sort of compromise. You can buy a cash value life insurance policy inside your traditional 401K defined contribution plan, such as a profit-sharing plan and a defined benefit plan. But keep in mind, as far as tax benefits are concerned, the traditional plan rules still supersede the life insurance tax benefits in terms of cash value withdrawal, but the death benefit is still income tax-free.

Rate of Return of Various Investments

There are two kinds of investments for wealth building: 1) Short-term and 2) Long-term.

The short-term wealth building investments are liquid assets, vehicles like checking accounts, savings accounts, money markets, and so forth, for your emergencies, opportunities, security, and overall peace of mind.

Before looking at the return of long-term savings and investments, let's understand the underlying premise for all long-term investments and why you are giving up current enjoyment of your income. The goal is to have a comfortable income stream in retirement and pass the leftover assets to family and/or charities in the most efficient way. It only makes sense then to understand how retirement income streams work so that you can direct the savings you are accumulating today in ways that potentially give you the highest income when you retire.

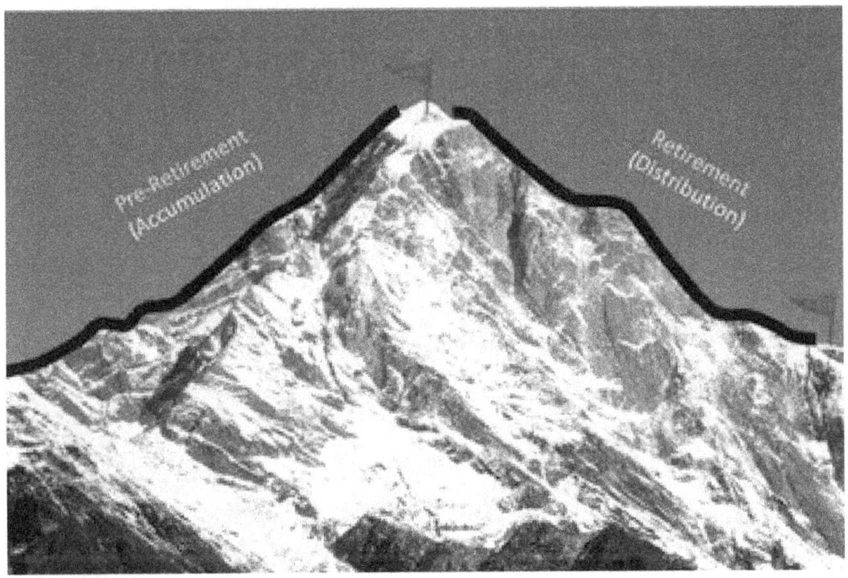

In other words, the economics of how retirement income streams work define how you should allocate your savings today. The sooner you get on an efficient path, the greater impact you will have in terms of results.

Two rates make up everyone's retirement income stream, and both are equally important. One is the accumulation rate – getting up the mountain. The other is the distribution rate – getting back down safely. Knowing how retirement income streams and distribution rates work is the basis for understanding how to save money in pre-retirement.

Accumulation Rate

In Chapter Five, I wrote about the three factors that affect your investment accumulation rate: 1) Asset allocation, 2) Taxation, and 3) Investment expenses.

There are three main asset classes for asset allocation: stocks, bonds, and cash. Three other asset classes have grown in popularity in the last few decades: real estate, commodities, and life insurance.

According to MeasuringWorth.com (a nonprofit organization advised by professors of top universities in the United States and Great Britain such as Harvard, Stanford, NYU, Vanderbilt, Oxford, and Northwestern), the annual growth rate of the Dow Jones Industrial Average (DJIA) since its inception on February 16, 1885 to February 28, 2019 is 5.14%. The annual growth rate of the S&P 500 since its inception on March 4, 1957 to February 28, 2019 is 6.92%, and of NASDAQ since its inception on February 5, 1971 to February 28, 2019 is 9.42%.

The following chart shows a comparison of the six main asset classes by the average long-term return, risk category, liquidity, and tax-efficient yield. The average expense ratio for actively managed mutual funds is between 0.5% and 1.0%, and typically goes no higher than 2.5%. For passive index funds, the typical ratio is approximately 0.2%. Expenses can vary significantly between different types of funds. The category of investments, the strategy for investing, and the size of the fund can all affect the expense ratio. With an average expense ratio of 1.25%, large-cap funds are typically less expensive than small-cap funds, which average 1.40%. Life insurance involves two kinds of policies here – whole life and indexed universal life. Both provide fixed interest and no expenses for managing the investment, but you do pay mortality and other administrative expenses.

Asset Class	Long Term Return	Risk	Liquidity	Taxable or Tax-free
Stocks	7%	Very High	Very Low	Taxable
Bonds	4%	Low	Medium	Taxable
Real Estate	6%	High	Very Low	Taxable
Cash	2%	No Risk	Very High	Taxable
Commod-ities	6%	Very High	Very Low	Taxable
Whole Life Insurance	4.5%	Low	Medium	Tax-free
S&P Index Universal Life Insur-ance	6.86%	Low	Medium	Tax-free

Distribution Rate

Fidelity suggests limiting retirement income withdrawal or distribution at 4% to 5 % of your savings/investments. That recommendation is largely in line with the 4% rule, a withdrawal regimen that traces its origins to a 1994 study by now-retired financial planner William Bengen. Essentially, Bengen tested a variety of withdrawal rates using historical rates of returns for stocks and bonds. He found that 4% was the highest withdrawal rate (even though you can earn a higher accumulation rate) retirees could use if they wanted their money to last at least 30 years, assuming they invested in the most optimal portfolio of 50% bonds and 50% stocks.

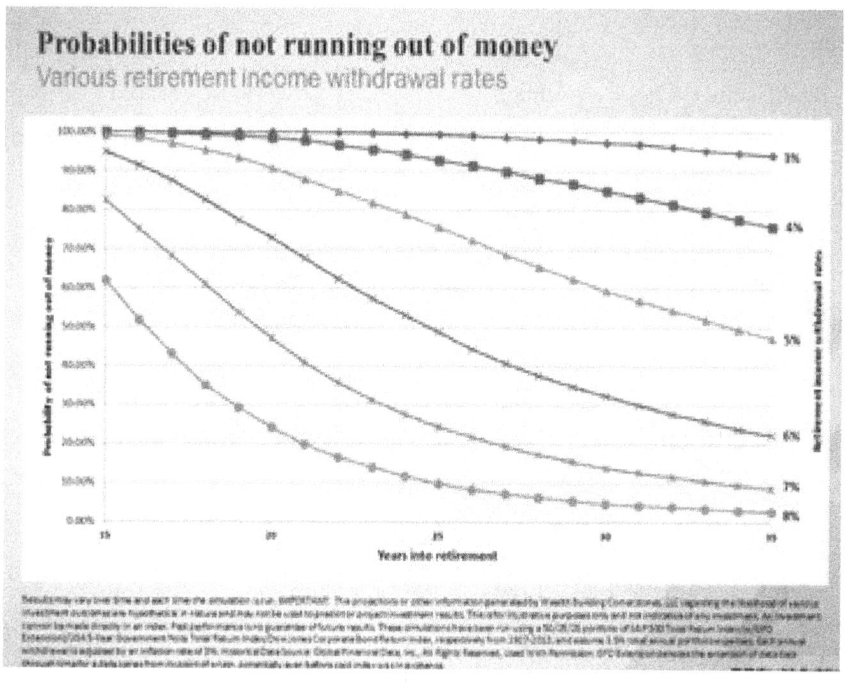

Probabilities of not running out of money
Various retirement income withdrawal rates

In recent years, however, a number of experts have challenged this rule, warning that it no longer offers the same level of assurance against running through one's assets than it did in the past. "The problem is that at today's low-interest rates, bonds can not provide the same level of income they previously did," says Wade Pfau, professor of retirement income at the American College of Financial Services, "That means investors have to rely more on the equity portion of their portfolio to support withdrawals." Since stock returns are highly volatile, if you withdraw more than you earn in a particular year, you have killed a portion of your working principle that will no longer be available when the stock market goes up.

The Economic Power of Combining Two Rates

The first economic power to work with is the "Fluctuating Rates of Return" power ,which can be a good accumulator of money. The second economic power is "Actuarial Science," which also can be a good distribution of power. These powers were always meant to work together in proper balance.

If you don't incorporate distribution power, then you can default to the 3-4% retirement income rate problem. When you incorporate Actuarial Science along the way, you put yourself on a path that can potentially provide higher retirement income rates from the assets you've built. The balance between these economic powers is the key. Having too much of either can make you less efficient. Then the power of actuarial science, through the death benefit and cash value of the whole life insurance or indexed universal life, can interact with the fluctuating interest rate power of retirement assets to create the ability to take higher retirement income rates safely. You need to be working towards building the proper balance between these two powers on your way to retirement.

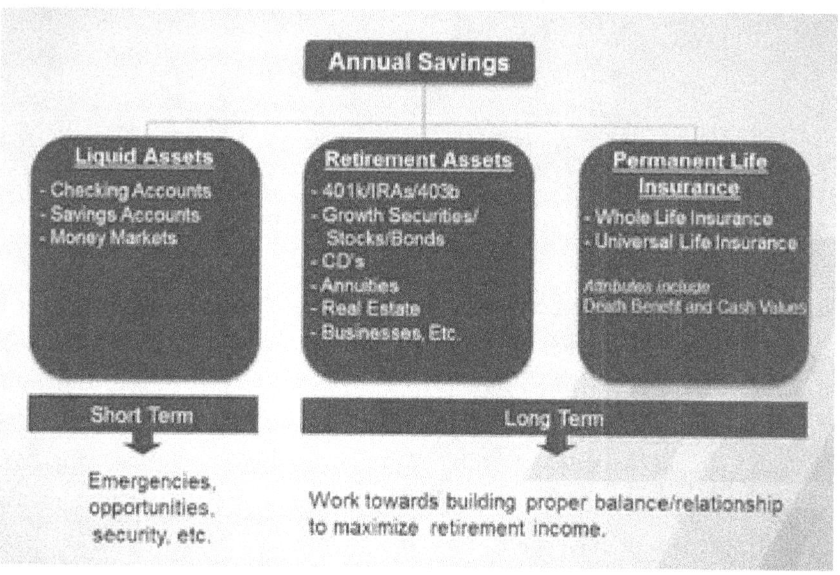

At the time of retirement, you must choose these two cornerstones, which are called "Covered Assets" for the exchange/trade option and "Volatility Buffer" for the investment option. A covered retirement asset is accompanied by an equal amount of a whole life insurance death benefit. Similar to how most government entities provide retirement pensions to their employees, covered retirement assets lay the foundation for self-made pensions in retirement. This is accomplished through the interaction of a retirement income tool called an "Income Annuity," which is a self-made pension, includes your whole life insurance death benefit, and is unrelated to the curves of the withdrawal rate simulations.

Under this option the interaction of your other retirement assets and cash value life insurance gives you the ability to create a guaranteed retirement paycheck for life. Historically this is in the range of 7% to 13% from the assets you've built, while at the same time providing perpetuation of retirement income for a spouse and/or a legacy for your heirs.

Over the past thirty years or so, the Internal Revenue Service has implemented various sections to their tax code to allow consumers to pick plans that work best for them. Section 7702 of the Internal Revenue code allows another option using the cash value of life insurance. Like a Roth IRA, there are no tax savings at the time of putting money into the plan, but there are advantages to the rest of the plan:

- No income tax upon withdrawal from the 7702 plan.
- No contribution limits to a 7702 plan.
- No penalties for withdrawal either at the federal or state level before age 59½.
- No required minimum distribution (RMD) at age 70½.
- No stock market risks to the 7702 plan.

The key here is that the 7702 plan is based on the actuarial science power that uses whole life insurance and indexed universal life insurance. With whole life, earnings within the plan are based on fixed interest, dividends, and compounding interest. This is done without stock market risks through strong, highly rated life insurance companies that have been successful in business for over 150 years. I have written in detail about various cash value life insurance in Chapter 10: The Dull nvestment of Life Insurance.

Summary

Remember, you get one shot at setting up and establishing your retirement plan. The 7702 plan can give you a strong building block for your retirement foundation. If you are healthy, you can take advantage of this plan. You can meet your family obligations, and maintain your lifestyle when your working days are behind you. With the 7702 plan, you can do this with a peace of mind since you are saving on a tax-deferred basis, while earning powerful returns without market risks.

Also, a 7702 plan allows you more flexibility than many other retirement plans because there are no restrictions on when you access your money, and you can do so without paying income tax on it. When you are figuring out how to diversify your investments and savings, this should be a component worth considering.

CHAPTER 13

College Savings for an Expensive Education

"Wealth can only be accumulated by the earnings of industry and the savings of frugality."

John Tyler

College is expensive. Not exactly a big secret there. The cost of a college education is constantly in the news. Its usual context is in how much money college graduates owe once they leave school and are out in the "real world."

In its most recent survey of college pricing, the College Board reports that a "moderate" college budget for an in-state public college for the 2018–2019 academic year averaged $26,670. A moderate budget at a private college averaged $48,510. Of course, you multiply this figure by four and add some inflation to get an idea of the total cost for college. If your child goes to a school above the "moderate" figure, you are looking at even more money. Obviously, this is for undergraduate studies. If your child wants to get a graduate degree in, say, medicine, law or finance, you are looking at an additional $60,000 per year. If your child attends a four-year medical school, multiply the annual cost by four and add some inflation. You get the picture. It's a serious endeavor for any family. At the same time, an education from a top college can be the best possible investment you can ever make in your life, giving security for life to your next generation.

Since you are probably just catching your breath from the figures I mentioned above, I need to point out that they do not include room and board, books, supplies, transportation to campus and personal expenses. I didn't want to shock you all at once. If current trends remain consistent, educational costs could potentially rise by 5% annually.

As a parent, you want the best for your children. You invest time into building your child's character and integrity, instilling in them core values that will hopefully stay with them through life. Many parents believe that if they spend the time preparing their children to face the world, it will be enough to make them successful and happy in their life.

A major component in this day and age is that without a good college education, many of these intuitive, gifted young people will never fully reach their potential. Business leaders today place a large and unprecedented value on having a quality education from an esteemed college or university. Twenty years ago, having a college degree may have helped a person get a promotion. Now you need a degree just to get through the company's front door.

Many parents today underestimate the huge financial commitment involved in financing a college education. It's important to start effective college saving strategies as soon as possible. For this reason, it is vital to start planning for your child's education when they are very young. A good rule of thumb might be to start during the time when each son or daughter (and if you're a grandparent, when your grandchild) is a baby!

As with any savings plan already covered in this book, all college savings plans or strategies are not created equal. The best plans offer lower expenses and special tax advantages to pay for college tuition. A smart college savings plan should allow you to legally "hide" your assets and help you qualify for financial aid, if you fall on the lower income side of the equation.

Saving for your child's college education requires a long-term commitment and sizable monthly or annual contribution to a plan or policy. In the same manner that you save for retirement, the earlier you start your plan, the better. The right college savings plan, structured in a tax-efficient manner and constructed during a child's younger years, will allow for college education choices to be determined by their grades and SAT or ACT scores, as opposed to which schools are most affordable or the scholarships they receive. As a side note, investing in the student's extra-curricular activities is also a very important part of college admission preparation.

Following are three of the most viable and popular college savings plans:

1. Bank CD or Money Market Account

2. 529 College Savings Plan

3. Cash Value Life Insurance-based College Savings Plan

The first plan is your basic savings plan. The amount you save will grow if you exercise discipline and put enough money away each month. However, you are paying taxes on the money you place into savings and you will be paying taxes on the annual interest your money earns. While you do not pay taxes on the money you withdraw from the plan, it is not the most efficient method to save for college. The only time this savings method is ideal is when you started saving for college very late, and you need money in the next couple years. At the time, the safety and liquidity of money is more important than tax advantages or higher earning you would receive with other plans.

One thing you discover when your child tries to secure financial aid for his education is that all of your assets are used in the calculation. The paradox is that the more you save for college, the less your child will be allowed to receive in financial aid.

A more efficient way to save for college is the 529 college savings plan. Congress created Section 529 plans in 1996, and they have emerged as one of the popular ways to save money for college. Section 529 plans are officially known as "qualified tuition programs" under federal law.

A 529 college savings plan or program is a college funding vehicle that has federal tax advantages. There are two types of 529 plans: college funding (or savings) plans and prepaid tuition plans. Although college funding plans and prepaid tuition plans share the same federal tax advantages, there are important differences between them.

Section 529 College Savings Plans

529 college savings plans let you save money for college in an individual investment account. Individual states run these plans, which typically designate an experienced financial institution to manage them. To open an account, you fill out an application, choose a beneficiary, and start contributing money. After this, you simply decide when, and how much, to contribute.

The plan investment managers commonly invest your money based on the age of your daughter or son (this is known as an age-based portfolio). Under this model, when a child is young, most of the portfolio's assets are allocated to aggressive investments. Then, as a child grows, the portfolio's assets are gradually and automatically shifted to less volatile investments to preserve principal. The idea is to take advantage of the stock market's potential for high returns when a child is still many years away from college, then to lessen the risk of these investments in later years. When it is time for college, the beneficiary can use the funds at any college in the US and abroad, as long as it is accredited by the U.S. Department of Education.

Section 529 Prepaid Tuition Plans

Prepaid tuition plans let you save money for college, too, but in a different way. Prepaid tuition plans may be sponsored by states (on behalf of public universities) or by private colleges. A prepaid tuition plan lets you prepay tuition expenses now for use in the future. The plan's money manager pools your contributions with those from other investors into one general fund. The fund assets are then invested to meet the plan's future obligations. Many plans even guarantee a minimum rate of return.

The most common type of prepaid tuition plan is a contract plan. With a contract plan, in exchange for your upfront cash payment (or series of payments), the plan promises to cover a predetermined amount of future tuition expenses at a particular college in the plan. These plans have different criteria for determining how much they'll pay out in the future. If your child ends up attending a school that isn't in the prepaid plan, you'll typically receive a lesser amount according to a predetermined formula.

There are definite advantages to 529 college savings plans. They are federal and state tax-deferred growth. The money you contribute to a state-sponsored qualified 529 plan is after taxed dollars, but it grows tax-deferred each year. Your earnings will be free of federal tax, as long as the money is used for college. Likewise, the money in a 529 plan receives favorable federal estate tax treatment. Your plan contributions are not considered part of your estate for federal tax purposes.

There are also state tax advantages. States can also add their own tax advantages to 529 plans. For example, some states exempt qualified withdrawals from income tax or offer an annual tax deduction for your contributions.

Section 529 plans are open to anyone, regardless of income level. It does not necessarily have to be opened by a parent. A grandparent, another relative, or any interested adult can set one up for a child. It also has a high contribution limit. The total amount you can contribute to a 529 plan is generally high. Most plans have limits of $250,000 and up.

While there are definite advantages to a 529 plan, it also has its potential downsides. These plans do not guarantee your investment return due to typical stock market volatility. You can lose some or all of the money you have contributed if you have made some serious wrong decisions about the investments. Even though prepaid tuition plans typically guarantee your investment return, some plans change the benefits they will pay out due to projected actuarial deficits.

There are penalties on non-qualified withdrawals. If you want to use the money in your 529 plan for something other than college, it will cost you. With a 529 college savings plan, you'll pay a 10% federal penalty on the earnings part of any withdrawal that is not used for college expenses (a state penalty may also apply). You will pay income tax on the earnings, too. With a prepaid tuition plan, you must either cancel your contract to get a refund or take whatever predetermined amount the plan will give you for a non-qualified withdrawal (some plans may make you forfeit your earnings entirely; others may give you a nominal amount of interest.)

There are typically fees and expenses associated with 529 plans. They might charge an annual maintenance fee, administrative fees, and an investment fee based on a percentage of your account's total value. Prepaid tuition plans may charge an enrollment fee and various administrative fees.

While 529 plans are efficient, its amount is included in the calculation of parents' assets when determining financial aid. You have to consider this downside, and the other potential liabilities of the 529 plan before deciding to take this track in a savings plan for college.

Cash Value Life Insurance Plan

Using cash value life insurance such as whole life and indexed universal life as a savings vehicle for college provides almost all the advantages of 529 college savings plans while eliminating some disadvantages.

Whole life insurance cash values receive pretty much the same favorable tax treatment as 529 plans. The money you put into life insurance is after tax dollars and the growth within the policy is tax-deferred. Utilizing policy loans, you can make tax-deferred loans to fund your child's college experience. The policy's cash values can be withdrawn as a policy loan without any tax consequences for any purpose and at any time. If you do not use the money for qualified college expenses, there is no 10% IRS penalty as there is with 529 plans.

This is a life insurance policy. Your family gets life insurance protection while also meeting the important financial goal of college financial planning. If you die prematurely, the death benefit is there to provide sufficient funds for your child's education at the college of his or her choice.

Life insurance allows you to include a waiver of premium rider for a very miniscule cost. This means that if you become totally disabled because of a sickness or injury, the insurance company will pay your life insurance premiums. Therefore, your college savings plan will be self-completing. No other plans will continue putting payments in for you if you cannot do so because of a disability.

In whole life insurance plans, you have the safety of a guaranteed cash value. You don't have to risk losing it in the stock market! When you start out the plan, you will know how much you will have in assets when the time comes to access the money for college. With indexed universal life, you will have the opportunity to invest in the stock market and take advantage of potential increases in value while limiting stock market losses with a zero percent return floor.

This plan is one of the few ways to legitimately "hide" assets when computing financial aid eligibility. Since life insurance values are not included in the federal methodology for calculating financial aid, you will not be penalized for saving money in this way for college.

A cash value life insurance plan has its owned drawback – it only works well if you start while the child is very young, unless you are trying to shelter your money for financial aid purposes.

Summary

It takes consistency and discipline to save the large amount of money needed for college. To be successful at it, parents need to formulate a plan early and stick with it. A traditional savings plan offers limited advantages. The 529 plan for college savings was implemented by the government to aid parents in setting money aside for college. It offers tax-deferred growth and limited tax liabilities when money is taken out for college. However, these plans are affected by market conditions, fees and expenses, and subject to heavy penalties if taken out early or not used for education.

Whole life insurance offers an attractive alternative with the same benefits as the 529 plan with additional advantages. It is not something that you include in your assets when applying for financial aid, the insurance company will continue paying your premiums if you become disabled, and you have greater flexibility with how you use your money.

Be sure to explore all the options of the available plans. You will need a great deal of money to put your children through college, so start early. The longer you wait, the more difficult it will be to meet your goals.

CHAPTER 14

Doubling Retirement Income

"The question isn't at what age I want to retire; it's at what income."

George Foreman

You have spent the last thirty or forty years working diligently at your chosen profession. You are successful and earned a reputation for being good at what you do. Throughout your working years, you saved meticulously for your retirement. The portfolio you established accumulated a great deal of money. A couple of investments did not go as well as you hoped, but overall, you did quite well. You own a nice home and have a vacation house at the beach. You traveled with your family and got your kids through college. They are doing well on their own, and you decide it is time to fold your tent.

Now what?

This is a question many people ask when they retire. The question covers a multitude of subjects. What are you going to do every day? Are you going to miss working? Is your spouse going to beg you to find something else to do? These are all very real issues you have to figure out. However, the most important situation you face is how to spend your money in order to get the most out of your savings and assets you have put together during your working years.

When it comes time to spending your savings at retirement, you need to have as much discipline and methodology to liquidate your money as you did when you were accumulating it. A very real problem that retirees face is outliving their money. This is a direct result of better medical care, nutrition and healthier lifestyles that have developed over the years.

One of your sources of income during retirement perfectly illustrates this point. You will be able to collect Social Security when you retire. When Franklin Roosevelt started the Social Security program in the early 1930s, life expectancy was only 62 years of age. If a person collected, the odds were that it wasn't going to be for a long time. Now, life expectancy is projected into the late '70s with many people hitting their 80s and 90s. Most of these people are not just sitting around waiting to die. They are out there being active in their communities, traveling and living life. It takes money to do that.

That is why you have to approach your retirement looking at the long-term ramifications. It is not unheard of for a successful professional to put in a good thirty years of work and retire at 55. The chances are good you have another 30 years of living to worry about!

When looking at the different savings plans, a successful professional like yourself at retirement will have accumulated a very nice nest egg through a diversified portfolio by following the suggestions in this book. You will be receiving Social Security, which is not much of a factor in the grand scheme of things. Let's review what you saved through your own initiatives.

When spending your savings, there are four factors you always have to consider. You need to know how the government requires you to report any disbursements of your portfolio on your income tax. Likewise, you should know what assets could have estate tax implications. Knowing what your rate of return is on each of your investments will also help you establish a priority on what monies to tap first. Finally, you have to take into account if any of your investments have a death benefit for your beneficiaries.

For our example here, let's say Dr. Sam was an excellent general practitioner and is retiring. Through his efforts working with various professionals, he has five buckets of savings to draw from in his retirement. They are:

1. CD's and savings accounts - $500,000

2. Brokerage account with investments in stocks, commodities, mutual funds, etc. - $1,000,000

3. Qualified retirement plans (IRA, defined benefit plan, defined contribution, etc.) - $2,000,000

4. Real Estate (primary home, vacation home) - $1,000,000

5. Whole life insurance - $1,000,000 cash value/$3,000,000 death benefit

I have listed these in the order in which Dr. Sam should withdrawal moneys to fund his retirement life. Follow along as I explain the rationale.

In bucket #1, the good doctor accumulated a half million dollars in various CDs and savings accounts. He already paid income tax on the money he originally put into these savings. He has also paid income tax every year on any interest the money earned. That interest is miniscule. He won't pay income tax on any of the money he takes out, the rate of return on his money is small, and whatever interest that is reportable every year will become lower the more he takes out. For these reasons, it makes sense that this is the first batch of money he takes for retirement. It doesn't increase his income taxes to withdraw these funds, as it reduces the size of his estate, and there is no death benefit attached to it.

Dr. Sam should then move on to his brokerage account. Like his savings, Sam used after-tax dollars to invest, and he has been paying income tax on any earnings and dividends over the years. His money earns more here than in his traditional savings accounts, so that is one reason to use this bucket second. Any withdrawals do not have to be reported on his income tax since they've been taxed already through the years. With no death benefit available here, this becomes bucket number two for him to take from.

The doctor's qualified retirement plans require different considerations. Remember, the money he put into these plans avoided income tax when invested. Likewise, the earnings and interest accumulated over the years were also not taxed. If the money was invested well, he should have had a decent rate of return over time. When he withdraws this money, he will have to report this on his current income tax.

Now you might think that with good earnings and knowing that it is reportable income when tapped, these retirement plans should be the last thing he wants to access. This is where the Internal Revenue Service comes in. Remember, Congress established the framework for these plans and worked them into the tax code of the IRS. Their creation was to encourage retirement savings for all of the reasons mentioned in previous chapters. When created, these plans had an Required Minimum Distribution (RMD) built into them. This means that when the doctor reaches 70 ½ years old, he has to start taking an income from his plans whether he needs it or not. It is the IRS's way of saying, "We let you exempt all this money from income tax for years. It's time to start paying up!" Ideally, it might be one of the last buckets of money the doctor wants to dip into, but at a certain point, he doesn't have a choice.

Real estate allows a person flexibility on what to do with it. In the doctor's case, he has two homes. For some people, they want to downsize their main home, while others want to keep it for the children and grandchildren to return to. Others buy the vacation home with the idea to sell the main home, and move permanently to the vacation home at retirement. It is all a matter of personal choice. Factors such as equity, property taxes, and location also come into play. A home is a big asset that can be accessed in the case of some catastrophic emergency and is usually one of the last buckets to utilize.

This brings us to the fifth and final bucket: whole life insurance. It should be the final bucket for several reasons. This is the one source of retirement income that has a death benefit. Remember the multitude of reasons for having whole life insurance as part of your balanced investment strategy. It provides for beneficiaries; it can pay for estate taxes; it takes care of final expenses, etc. Whole life insurance covers a variety of concerns.

Also, remember that whole life insurance builds up a cash value over the life of the policy. If you need to access the cash value, you can do so by taking loans from the policy. This means you don't have to pay income tax on it. In our example, Dr. Sam has a $3 million policy with a million dollars of cash value. Even if Dr. Sam takes out an entire one million dollars and then passes away, his beneficiaries will still receive $2 million!

When planned out properly, whole life insurance is there to wrap up all of your investments and provide for your family when you pass away. It gives you the luxury to use up all other investments, and still provide a legacy for your loved ones. It even allows you to utilize the equity in your house for your retirement purposes through a reverse mortgage. Because of the death benefit of life insurance, your family can use that money to free the house after you die.

Doubling Your Retirement Income

You now understand that the purpose of any long-term savings or investment is to create retirement income, liquidity, and a legacy for the family. The more efficient you are at satisfying the desired income stream, the more money you will have left over for liquidity and leaving an inheritance for the family. So, what do you do with the money that you are not using to create the retirement income stream? From the visual perspective, think of this as a waterfall effect – you first need to use the available investments to satisfy your income objective then the remaining resources flow like a waterfall down into your liquidity and legacy functions.

For your retirement income, it is important to prepare for funds to last closer to life potential than just to life expectancy. Many people will live past life expectancy. Keeping this in mind, let's understand the products and methods available to utilize for your retirement income purposes.

Retiree Economic Rules

1. Income, Liquidity, and Legacy are the 3 functions of money in retirement.
2. Income is the first function of retirement to satisfy.
3. The more efficient we are at satisfying the desired income stream, the more money is generally left over for Liquidity/Legacy.
4. We are defining liquid (accessible) money in retirement as money not being used to create an income stream.
5. Liquidity is also Legacy in retirement.

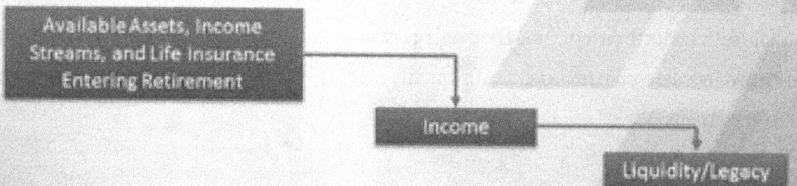

Available Assets, Income Streams, and Life Insurance Entering Retirement

Income

Liquidity/Legacy

Let's investigate how income from Dr. Sam's fluctuating return investment assets work in retirement, such as his brokerage account and qualified retirement assets (IRA, defined benefit plan, defined contribution, etc.). A potential problem Dr. Sam will encounter is how these assets react to the fluctuating rate of return when money is being withdrawn for retirement income. Let's take an example of his $1 million brokerage account.

Assume Dr. Sam happened to be on the right side of the stock market history and retired somewhere between 1970 to 1999 when the S&P 500 produced an average return of 14.84%. If Dr. Sam only withdraws 10%, that is $100,000 a year of his $1 million brokerage account. You can see that his account grew even after withdrawing $100,000 for 30 years.

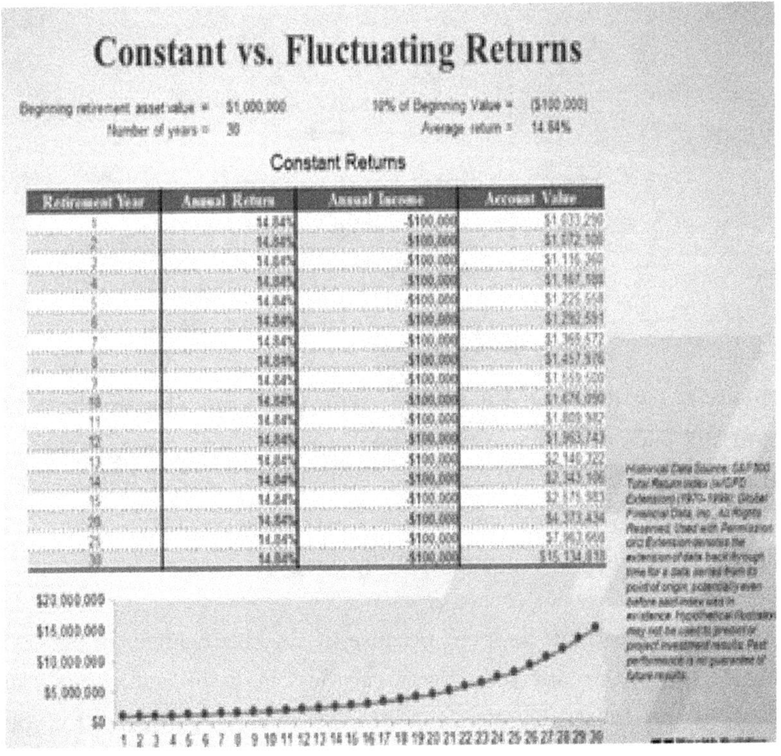
Constant vs. Fluctuating Returns

Beginning retirement asset value = $1,000,000 | Number of years = 30 | 10% of Beginning Value = ($100,000) | Average return = 14.84%

Constant Returns

Retirement Year	Annual Return	Annual Income	Account Value
1	14.84%	-$100,000	$1,033,296
2	14.84%	-$100,000	[illegible]
3	14.84%	-$100,000	$1,116,360
4	14.84%	-$100,000	[illegible]
5	14.84%	-$100,000	$1,226,558
6	14.84%	-$100,000	$1,292,591
7	14.84%	-$100,000	$1,365,572
8	14.84%	-$100,000	$1,447,976
9	14.84%	-$100,000	[illegible]
10	14.84%	-$100,000	[illegible]
11	14.84%	-$100,000	[illegible]
12	14.84%	-$100,000	$1,963,743
13	14.84%	-$100,000	$2,140,722
14	14.84%	-$100,000	$2,343,106
15	14.84%	-$100,000	[illegible]
20	14.84%	-$100,000	[illegible]
25	14.84%	-$100,000	[illegible]
30	14.84%	-$100,000	[illegible]

Here is the actual return of the S&P 500 from 1970 to 1999. So, if you add all these annual positive and negative yields during these thirty years and divide by thirty, then the average yield of 14.84% is the result. Now you are going to see how to take the fluctuating positive and negative yields and put them in the same table above and see what happens.

Constant vs. Fluctuating Returns

Range of years = 1970-1999 Average return = 14.84%

History of the S&P 500

Year	Annual Return	Year	Annual Return
1970	3.99%	1985	31.66%
1971	14.33%	1986	18.60%
1972	18.94%	1987	5.17%
1973	-14.79%	1988	16.61%
1974	-26.54%	1989	31.69%
1975	37.25%	1990	-3.10%
1976	23.67%	1991	30.47%
1977	-7.39%	1992	7.62%
1978	6.44%	1993	10.08%
1979	18.35%	1994	1.32%
1980	32.27%	1995	37.58%
1981	-5.05%	1996	22.96%
1982	21.48%	1997	33.36%
1983	22.50%	1998	28.58%
1984	6.15%	1999	21.04%

When you put the annual fluctuating return into the table on the next page, you still have the same average yield over the thirty years. However, instead of having close to fifteen million dollars at the end of thirty years, Dr. Sam is down to zero dollars between years thirteen and fourteen. It's eye-popping, and the question comes, "Why does this happen?"

This decrease in funds happens because of the rule changes in the distribution of income. In any year, if you earn less than you pulled out, you just killed off the dollars that were supposed to be earning a return for you in the next year. So, if you are going to try to use fluctuating return assets to provide retirement income, then the question becomes how would you go about determining what is a safe withdrawal rate?

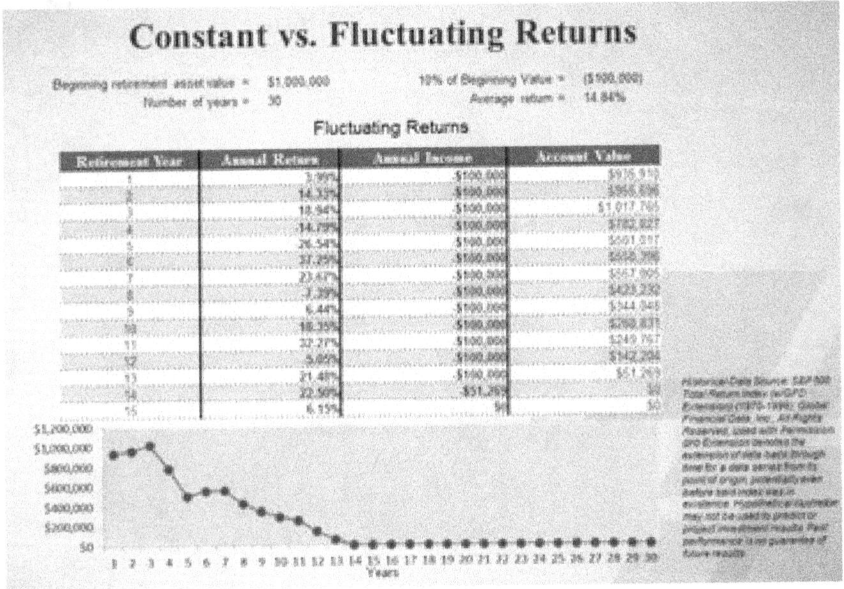

Retirement Year	Annual Return	Annual Income	Account Value
1	3.99%	$100,000	[illegible]
2	14.33%	$100,000	[illegible]
3	18.94%	$100,000	$1,017,765
4	14.79%	$100,000	[illegible]
5	26.54%	$100,000	[illegible]
6	37.25%	$100,000	[illegible]
7	23.47%	$100,000	[illegible]
8	7.39%	$100,000	[illegible]
9	6.44%	$100,000	[illegible]
10	18.35%	$100,000	[illegible]
11	32.27%	$100,000	$249,767
12	5.05%	$100,000	$142,204
13	21.48%	$100,000	$51,269
14	22.50%	$51,269	$0
15	6.15%	$0	$0

A software program called Monte Carlo simulations tries to answer this question by using the rates of return for all types of investment vehicles over the last 100 years or so to calculate the historical probabilities of running out of money in the retirement years based on the withdrawal rate. These programs run thousands of simulations for every 15, 20, 25, 30 and 35 year rolling time periods, taking into account all types of market conditions and interest rate environments.

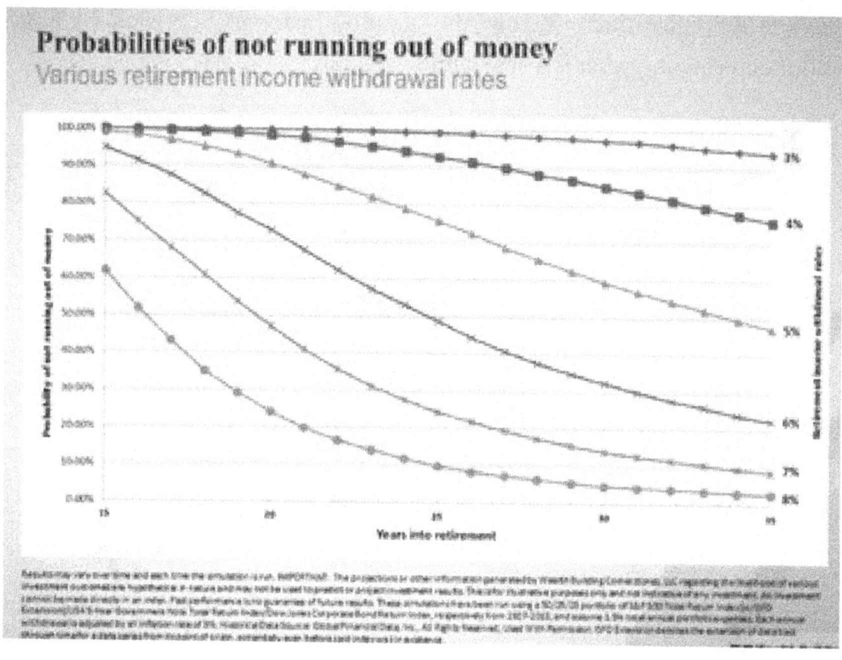

Let's take a look at the results of these simulations conceptually. This chart shows the historical probabilities of not running out of money years into retirement based on the withdrawal rate chosen at the beginning of retirement. It is important to understand that these are withdrawal (distribution) rates and not interest (accumulation) rates on your money in retirement. These simulations and curves exist because of the income withdrawal rate is established before knowing the fluctuating returns you will earn on your money.

As an example, let's say you choose an 8% withdrawal rate on your beginning retirement asset balance. This would put you on the bottom line. Thirty years into retirement, historically there is about a 5% chance of not running out of money and around a 90% chance of running out of money. So, it doesn't take a rocket scientist to tell you that by lowering your withdrawal rate, you'll have a better chance of not running out of money. Most financial experts agree using between a 3 to 4% withdrawal rate protects you from running out of money in retirement.

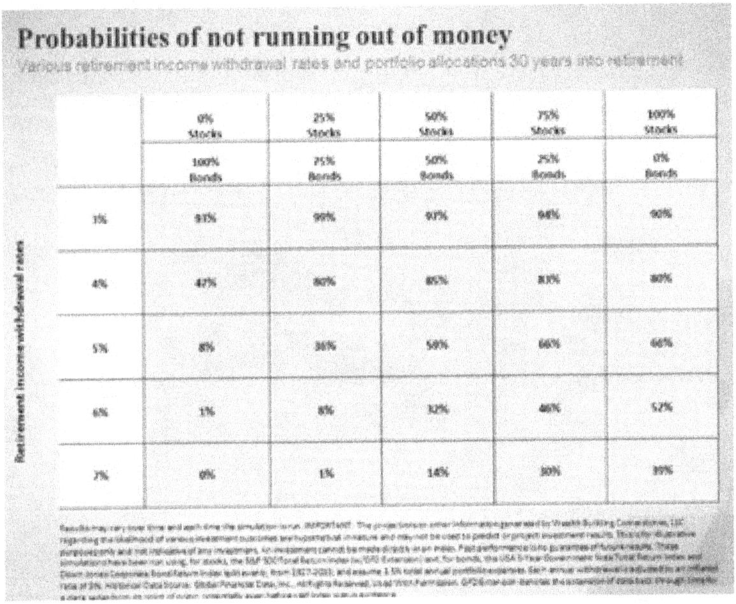

Probabilities of not running out of money

Various retirement income withdrawal rates and portfolio allocations 30 years into retirement

Retirement income withdrawal rates	0% Stocks / 100% Bonds	25% Stocks / 75% Bonds	50% Stocks / 50% Bonds	75% Stocks / 25% Bonds	100% Stocks / 0% Bonds
3%	93%	99%	97%	94%	90%
4%	47%	80%	85%	83%	80%
5%	8%	36%	59%	66%	66%
6%	1%	8%	32%	46%	52%
7%	0%	1%	14%	30%	39%

This previous chart was based on a 50/50 stock/bond allocation mix because it is generally one of the better performing mixtures throughout history, but you could choose a different allocation mix as well when running these types of simulations.

So, how can Dr. Sam double his retirement income by doubling the distribution rate without the risk of running out of the money later on? This can be done by combining two economic powers: 1) Fluctuating interest rate power and 2) Actuarial science power. The first power is to earn returns using the short-term fluctuating interest rates by the related investment vehicles such as stocks, bonds, etc. This power is generally characterized by the fluctuating returns on risk/reward based outcomes. The second power you can utilize to earn returns is the power of actuarial science provided by insurance-related investment vehicles. This power is generally characterized by a steadier return over time that doesn't fluctuate as much and can be guaranteed. These two powers can be a good complement to one another when used together in a balanced approach.

As you get closer to retirement, begin to put together a strategy for when

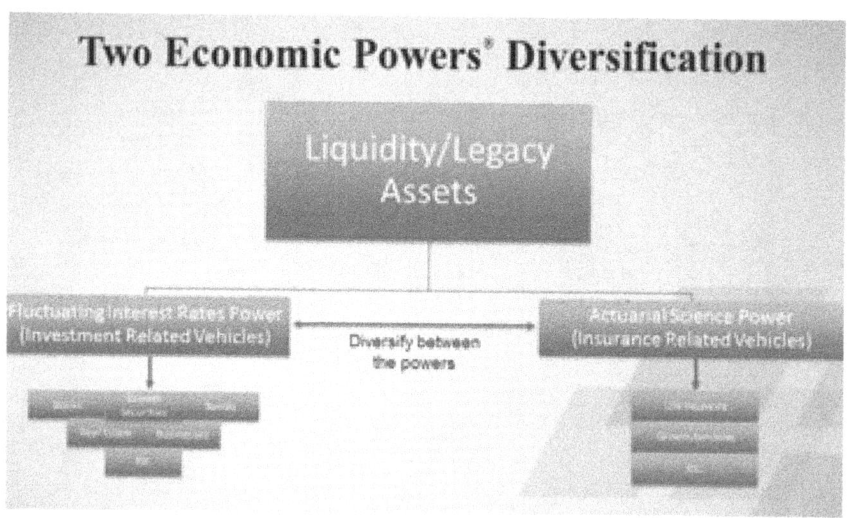

you are done working. As you can see, you need to plan how to spend your money as much as you planned when saving it. It would not do to agonize over all your investments and then spend it too quickly due to a bad game plan.

This book's purpose is to give you a simple, but comprehensive overview of how you can realize significant tax savings now while preparing for your future. You now know what kind of professionals you need to look for to optimize both your current tax savings and your retirement. If nothing else, I want you to be able to start asking the right questions about what will work for you.

I always go on the premise that you worked hard to get to where you are in life. You should be allowed to keep as much of your hard-earned money as possible. If you do not take care of yourself, who will?

For updates, more reports, and
additional financial advice, please visit:
www.NeilJesani.com

www.ingramcontent.com/pod-product-compliance
Lightning Source LLC
Chambersburg PA
CBHW071416210326
41597CB00020B/3532